Never Look Back! You Are Not Going That Way!

The Path to Real Professionalism

ALPER KUL

COPYRIGHT © 2018 ALPER KUL
All rights reserved.
Never Look Back! You Are Not Going That Way: *The Path to Real Professionalism*
ISBN-10: 1975732677
ISBN-13: 9781975732677
Published by Create Space.

Praise for *Never Look Back!*

"A delightful blueprint for personal career development taking the reader on a contemporary journey with a fluent, coherent, and sincere dialogue interactively; giving diverse references to credible and authorized resources blended into the morally justified flow of the circumstances. The synopsis is a must read the illustrious book of today opening clear vision for the future."

- Fahhan Özçelik, Senior Independent Consultant, Strategic Business Development in FMCG & Food-Service

"Most important decisions in one's life are the choices for the career and marriage partner. Alper Kul has done a great job of opening one's mind about the career choice and balanced Life. The choice of dialogue as the style of delivery makes the book easy to read and understand. Well done..."

- Dr. Yılmaz Argüden, Chairman of ARGE Consulting & Founder of Argüden Governance Academy"

"A fresh and impressive look at managing your own career:" Never Look Back! You Are Not Going That Way!" should be required reading for all business managers, academicians and new generation employees"

- Osman Ünal, Chief HR Officer at Ekol Logistics

"Alper Kul's book, "Never Look Back! You Are Not Going That Way", provides insight on the mind, body and soul of a potential career journey in a completely fresh format. Its conversational style engages your mind. It's personal questioning challenges your body. And it's holistic nature satiates your soul. In today's information age we face two dilemmas. The first is that we can do anything we want, but ultimately we can't do everything. Choices must be made. The second is that the pace of change in the future of jobs is going to keep increasing exponentially and will feature new career opportunities that have never existed before. How we deliberately design a life we love is not a luxury, but a necessity. The heart of this book is about mindfulness. And mindfulness should be explored and strengthened as a core competency by all."

- Didem Altop, Endeavor Turkey,
Co-Founder & Managing Director

"Never look back! You are not going that way!" sincerely brings carefully selected titles from life to the attention of readers in a humble way. Through the following pages, you feel that sincerity derives from the real life experiences of the author. Transitions of generations are one of the most current topics in today's world. For the ones who are the representatives of generation X, like me, we feel a little uncomfortable working together with "Generation Y". After having attended many discussions and analyzing various resources on this topic, I found the book very successful when it comes to bringing a blissful attitude regarding the transition of generations and bringing two sides on a common ground. Alper's 5 wings windmill presents 5 factors of personal development; sports, career, social, art and intellectualness. Those wings, spinning in the same direction, generates personal development which creates successful organizations, communities, and countries at the end by the qualities of those individuals. In addition to those skills, the book presents successful business representatives which I believe their common skill is successful communication which can't be measured but is a crucial element reaching the target. The book "Never look back! You are not going that way!"

takes its place in literature as a very blissful and useful guide for the ones who are preparing himself/herself to the future, who are looking for a direction. A must read and needs to be recommended!

- Güray Karacar, Tofaş Turkish Automotive Company- External Relations Director

"There are wrong things which we consider as true. Mostly, we can't realize them. When we get into trouble, just then we understand the truth. Especially the young who have just started their career path will find the information which is necessary to reduce their mistakes as much as possible. Not only with its pure revelation but also with the clearest way in expression. That is the reason why I strongly recommend this book in the seminars for students. In today's most challenging world, it is one of the books which young people have to read."

- Ali Özel, Senior Consultant at SAN Consultancy

"The book starts with human resources, but in the following pages, it defines human not as a kind of resource to be consumed but an individual value. As a matter of fact, Alper helps everyone to discover, face and then reveal their own value they already possess. You may call it career, success, happiness or whatever you like. That's why it is crucial for young people to read it. Also with its name which points out always moving forward, it tells everyone not to look back, but to move on as the most proper way. I think Alper definitely tells the truth."

- Ömer Aykul, Lawyer of Ecology and Environment

"While trying to develop robots to replace them with humans, we did a great job in many areas. But we couldn't succeed one thing which is developing human soul and emotion. It won't even happen in the future and by this way, humanity will be our most precious value in all ages. While the shape of human resource in public has been interchanging rapidly due to developing technologies, the ones who can pay attention to this voice which says "Don't look back!" will be fortunately seated in the train of change. Thank you very much, Dear Alper Kul..."

- Bülent Ünsever, Co-Founder & CEO at Blue Ocean Robotics, Turkey

"In this book that I found literal, flowing and escapist, you will discover not only the path to a successful career but also the main tips to be "A Happy Individual" as well."

- Ozan Çiçek, President of Knorr-Bremse CVS Turkey and the Middle East

"Alper Kul takes complex career selection, successful managers' profiles, updated workplace information and makes them truly accessible to the developing professional. It presents material in engaging, concise prose and provides excellent and relevant examples. This book will appeal not only to those aiming for business success and personal growth, but also targets oriented young brains. I congratulate the author on this eminently thoughtful, useful and practical book."

- Arzu Toktay, Financial Advisor and Strategist

"Non-repetitive matters, direct results with no work around straight through to call to action by changing behavior. Good job!"

- Tulu Akyol, Head of IT Governance & Strategy

"Unlike the classical books which appear when you look for one written for personal development, changing your eye-view on life with its attitudes from different points, being full of illustrations that contribute inspiration and excitement, guiding you on the way you should follow, this book qualifies its title as much as possible."

- Murat Denge, Managing Director at DENGE Airport Equipment

"5 Wings Windmill: Career, Art, Intellectuality, Social, Sports. Life is a sum of values you added to yourself and your surrounding. The more balanced the values on the 5 vanes of the windmill the more happy and successful you are in your life. People usually tend to forget the 5 wings of the windmill of their lives and pretend to focus on one of them which makes their lives miserable at the end. Unfortunately, the moment a person realizes this fact is most of the time too late that the person cannot return. In this book of mind, reality, hope, and love; Alper makes us face this reality and gives a big hand for change and refreshment for the rest of our lives. You will enjoy learning how to improve your motivation power along with your strategic intelligence which will lead you to your ultimate happiness in your life. I wish I could have read this book 20 years ago however I still look forward as I am not going back..."

- Murat Zahal, Senior Consultant at Zahal Consulting

"I am very impressed by the book as it seemed, in a way, like a guide for our youth in identifying their career path in a very complicated environment. It helps them to improve their techniques of determining the right track in a huge career forest, where the global insights do not overlap with our newly revised culture, geography, and political gaps. With a 360 degree outlook, the book warns them about the mismatch of the local and global expectations and enlightens them with the correct alternatives."

- Yaprak Metin, Executive Counsellor to the Board

"The theme of the new millennium is not about how strong you are. It is about your ability to adapt to change. If you translate this piece of information into the language of career management, your contemporary competencies become more important than your previous ones. If you scan through this book you may notice the word "career" taking part many pages. Please do not be mistaken that the book is targeting new graduates. Wherever you are, on your career journey you will find something worth reading in this book. Of course, the new graduates will find plenty of useful information, the golden rules of work life and priceless career paths and maps. You will also find some sophisticated data that is very well analyzed and searched. Mr. Career has added his personal interpretation of the data as well. All the crises we have been going through, economical or otherwise, have a certain effect not only on generation Y but also the members of X. May be you should read the book only for this reason. That's how you can find your own ways to adapt and live with change. Not to look back! (because that's not the way to go) but to take us on a trip to horizons. Thank you, Mr. Career."

-Tulga Onay, HR Professional, Coach & Mentor

The book "Never Look Back! You're Not Going That Way!" in which Alper Kul, one of the most important businessmen and "The Agent of Change", objectively looked through management perceptiveness and HR culture in Turkey has the feature of being the most extensive and the most different work I have read recently in terms of stressing upon the added-value of a human and quality oriented system. I especially advise this book to the newbies in business World as it guides about career trends through Turkey's most leading 5 businessman's career path, expertness, and gaining vision. I believe the first step on the path to success should always be the vision that is well determined. When decisions made through this vision are put in progress at the right time, at right workpieces, with right labor, and the quality production concept, then success is not a surprise. Through Turkey's goal to be one of the strongest economies in the World, I also adopted a management concept which is organizational, sustainable, and able to pass down through generations in my company. In this regard, I believe this book is reminding and inspirational at creating a human oriented attitude.

- Orhan Turan, Chairman of the Board / ODE Insulation

Dear Alper, I honestly loved the book and the holistic approach you brought to the table with questions to be considered for today and the future of a nation's workforce challenged with the facts of local, global trends and forces shaping us. Your quest for how we will transform for the future leadership starting from today where we are challenged every day with new advancements with the fact that tomorrow is closer than we think brought the other level of provocating thought leadership. Excellent Job.

> - Can Buyukalkan, Global Projects Recruitment Director at Talent Club & Careerspot

About The Author

Alper Kul
Graduated from Italian High School and then as the first graduate from the department of International Relations within the Faculty of Economics and Administrative Sciences in Koç University, Alper Kul started his business life as front-office boy and receptionist in the Italian vacation village Sarıgerme Valtur in 1992. During the years 1993-1999, he worked in the textile industry as an interpreter in Italian and a sales assistant in different cities in Turkey. Besides, he served in a project to found the company in Italy for TIRSAN, the leading organization of trailer. Working as the field sales coordinator in Bridgestone Co. Between the years 2002-2004, Alper Kul became responsible for the markets in Italy, Spain, Lebanon, North Cyprus and Slovenia. At the same time, he was also responsible for the coordination of EXSA UK (London) and other markets.

In 2005-2012, he worked as the export manager for PepsiCo International, he was responsible for sales of Pepsi, Pepsi Light, Seven Up, Yedigün, Fruko, Lipton Ice Tea over Germany, Iraq, Kazakhstan, Azerbaijan, Turkmenistan, and all European countries and he was in charge of expanding the sales volume for abroad.

In order to support his personal and career development beyond his success in his business life, Alper Kul attended in a number of programs such as "Spanish Courses" in Istanbul Technical University, "Superior Sales Management" by Brian Tracy Institute, Management Simulation Program. He speaks English and Italian in the advanced level, Spanish in intermediate level and German in elementary level. He also got Latin language classes in Italian

High School for 4 years. As the founder and the general coordinator of many social development groups, our author has also been into the music and he is composing in new age style.

By considering himself as **"An Agent of Change"**, Alper Kul created a climax in thousands of people's career and lives through all his seminars and training.

About The Translator

Ayşe Özbay Erozan
After graduating from Robert College and Boğazici University, she attended the University of Michigan, Ann Arbor, for her master's studies in anthropology. Translation has been a constant in her life ever since 2002. She enjoys a refined appreciation of Baroque music, crime novels, and modern Turkish literature.

More about the author and his works
in various fields

- **Personal Web And Social Pages:**
  twitter.com/alperkulpro
  instagram.com/alperkulpro
  fb.com/alperkulmusic
  fb.com/alperkulpro (official author fb page)

- **Music:**
  fb.com/alperkuljazz
  alperkulmusic.com
  reverbnation.com/alperkuljazz
  fb.com/groups/alperkulcomposer
  youtube.com/alperkul

- **TV Programs and Seminars, Music Videos:**
  Youtube.com/alperkul

- **Career:**
  fb.com/groups/baykariyer
  fb.com/baykariyer

- **Pro:**
  Alperkul.pro

- **Development Groups:**
  Gelisimgrubu.org
  Besiktasgelisim.org

In the memory of Mustafa Koç

Mustafa Vehbi Koç
(29 October 1960, Ankara - 21 January 2016, Istanbul),
He was one of the most important Turkish businessmen.
Mr. Koç was the chairman of the board in Koç Holding between
the years 2003-2016.

CONTENTS

International Edition Preface
Preface: We Have a Human Resource Problem

1. THE FIVE-WINGED WINDMILL MODEL • 19

    Socrates' Defense
    To Know Ourselves
    Our Wings
    Career / Sports / Intellectual / Art / Social
    Does Having a Career Mean Making a lot of Money?
    What Is a Career?
    Arab Spring
    Unemployment Among Young Adults
    We're on a Ship without a Compass!
    Where Does the Colony of Ants Live?
    The World's Youth Are Rising Up
    The Crises that Don't Want to Stop
    The Legend of Samsung
    They Work "Smart"
    What Is the Market? Does Anyone Know?
    Europe Has a Flat Tire
    The European Union Was Poorly Designed
    Without the Unemployment of Young Adults, It's Impossible
    The Third World War Started a Long Time Ago
    This World Only but Only a World of Hope
    Our People Are Without Hope
    There Isn't Just One Europe

A Universal Culture Is Essential
　　The Mediterranean Means Unemployment
　　The Northern Countries Have Outscored
　　Real Development Happens with Humanitarian Development

2. **THE FIRST TRUTH:**
   Time and "Timing" Management • 49

　　What Does It Mean to Come Out of the Cave?
　　The Way to Be Successful in Your Job Is to Go Beyond Being a Real Professional
　　Who Is the Professional?
　　Have You Ever Thought About What Education Is?
　　To Be Wise Is to Be Strategic
　　Time and "Timing" Management
　　The First Thirty Years in a Person's Life Are Very Critical
　　Now Is the Time to Start Thinking Like a Developed Society
　　Who Is "Vilfredo Frederico Damaso Pareto"?
　　The Pareto Principle in Time Management
　　The 80/20 Rule
　　The Parkinson Principle in Time Management
　　Foundational Principles

3. **THE SECOND TRUTH: Specialization • 65**

　　Work Life Is Relentless
　　The Certificate Legend
　　What Is CISSP?
　　The First Five Years of a Career Are Critical
　　The Goal Is a Consciously Dynamic Process
　　We Must Make Ourselves Think Like a Pilot

4. **THE THIRD TRUTH:**
   Communication, Relationships Management, and Social Intelligence • 71

　　Who Is the Disciplined Person?
　　The Most Basic Skill is Communication
　　In the End, The Workforce Is Waiting for a "Result" from You
　　Virtual Ignorance

Facebook or Twitter?
A Career in Social Media
"LinkedIn" Is Very Different from the Others
Head Hunter's Databases Have Been Outdated for Quite Some Time Now, and In Fact, Have Been Thrown Out
Without Qualified Internet Usage in Your Life Finding a Good Job Is Left to Chance
White Collared Workers Don't Give the Slightest Value to Workers
Sometimes It's to End a Relationship
The Most Important Effective Professional the Country Has Raised Is the Coca Cola Company's Administrative Board President Muhtar Kent
Muhtar Kent is a World Professional
Empowering Women Entrepreneurs
Muhtar Kent: Why I Am a Feminist?
Muhtar Kent Receives Water Leader Award
Who is Muhtar Kent?
July 2008 Coca Cola Put Kent in the Top Position
An Eight-Armed Octopus
The Turkish Schindler
Lesson 1: There Isn't a Universal Template
The Most Important Information is Attained First Hand
Lesson 2: To Work with the Right Person
To Be Able to Learn While Taking Risks
Manager in Title, Not in Person
Lesson 3: To Establish Long-Lasting Relationships
One Becomes a Professional Then a Leader
To Lead a Large Company as If It Were Small
Two Essential Duties for a Leader in Order to Never Be Replaced

5. WOULD YOU LIKE TO TRAVEL TO THE HORIZON? • 99

The First Key on the Horizon Journey is to Not Be an Ordinary Person

Rahmi Koç is a World Citizen
The Second Key on the Horizon Journey: To Write an Authentic Resume
Curriculum Vitae Et Studorium
Be Careful of Knowledge Pollution
One Day We Will Only Write Contribution Statements!
Everyone Can Have a Great Career!
American Writers Are Confessing that the American Dream Has Ended
The Information Age Is Full of Disorder and Ambiguity
Y Generation
Six Foundational Points
What Information Brings Me Closer to Finding a Job?
Get a Hold of Successful People's Resumes
What are HR Managers Impressed With?
The First Page
A CV Must be Short and Clear
It's Very Important to Work in Civil Society Organizations
In the Future, We Will Be Forced to Serve in the Civil Society Organizations
Resumes According to Their Types

6. TO RIDE THE CAREER TRAIN • 125

Choosing a Career Field is Life's Most Important Decision
Professionals' and Investors' Expectations May Be Different
In This World, The Word "To Know" Is an Incorrect Word
Number One Wagon: The Health Sector
The Obesity Problem
Health Care Companies Are Becoming a Community
The Most Critical Areas for Health Care Systems Management Are at the Top
Medical Shortfall and Operational Shortfall
Other Trend's Wagons
Overall Quality Has Already Been Shelved
Are Bankers Happy?
Security Systems in Banking

Financial Consulting Will Become Very Important
The Six Different Colors of Professional Groups
In America Career Life and Development Analysis Is Taken Seriously
"Best Jobs in America"
Marketing Has Lost its Old Magic
Products Have Ceased Being Products
Social Marketing Will Be a New Field
Without Knowing Psychology, You Can't Do Marketing
To be Professional Exporter!
There Is No Room for the Word "Love" in Your Work Life
Environmentalism is Mostly a Governmental Policy
A Smart Society Is One That Learns from Experience

7. WHAT IS "REAL" POWER? • 156

Motivation Has Four Stars
To Think Like Leonardo Da Vinci
Viktor Frankl and "The Frankl Dimension"
In Life, There's One Thing You Can Never Take from Someone
"Goal Consciousness" Is the Name of One Tactic in the Struggle
Small Goals Often Tire Someone as much as Large Goals
The Strength of Your Beliefs Determines How Strong Your Spirit Will Be
Life and Goals Need to Be Put in a Pyramid
Strategically Thinking on Only 111 Pages
Mind Mapping and The Strength of Creative Thinking
Great Thinkers Receive High Marks
Computers Alone Aren't Enough
The Romans Frequently Were Doing "SOLVITAS PERAMBULUM"!
The End Is Apparent: It's Two
We Must Be Certain of Our Actions
Everyone Likes Brave Person!
Break up the Complex!

8. THE REAL PROFESSIONALS • 176
   You Could Come Across Them at Any Place.
   "Dr. Oz" Is Actually a Communications Professor
   "Forbes" Placed Him Third in the Most Influential Person List for 2011
   Dr. Oz Is a Great Civil Society Leader
   The Dorm Room Diet
   Dr. Rıza Kadılar Is an Amazing Communicator and Civil Society Participant
   We are in the Presence of a Fantastic Professional!
   Reading Biographies
   A Smart Society Is One That Learns from Experience
   We Must Identify the Turkish Hawking
   Onur Güntürkün and "Vitality"
   A Child Named Onur
   Time, Expertise, Social Intelligence
   He is a "Snow Leopard"
   Nasuh Mahruki Has a Michael Jordan Spirit
   The Homeland Is Loved with Actions Not Words
   Never Look Back! You Are Not Going That Way!

Epilog (Professor Türker BAŞ) • 204

ADDITIONAL SECTIONS

1. EMPLOYMENT IN TURKEY, UNEMPLOYMENT AND THE INFORMAL ECONOMY • 208
   Turkish Statistical Institute
   We Have an Ombudsman! Does Anyone Know?
   Independent and Public Audit Authorities Need to Move from Ankara
   Knock Out Unemployment
   The Status of Women in Turkey
   We Are Last in Line Concerning Women in the Workforce
   OECD Is a Litmus Test
   The Percentage of Labor Force Participation Is the Measure
   We Are among the Last Concerning Labor Force Participation

If Only Turkey's Labor Force Participation Were Up to the OECD Average What Happened to Our Unemployment Numbers?
The Woman Labor Force Scene Isn't Encouraging
"Informal Economy" Is the Root of All Evil

2. THE WORK LIFE CONSISTS OF PROCEDURE! • 227

What Does It Mean to Work at Büyükdere Street?
To Work at the Headquarters Means to Work at Büyükdere Street
Plaza Cult!
This World Is a Procedure World, This Country Became a Country of Procedures
We All Become Robots!
We Became a Depressive Case
Whether You Work or Not, You're in Depression!
The Situation Is Grave...

"When I went to school, they asked me what I wanted to be when I grew up. I wrote down 'happy'. They told me I didn't understand the assignment, and I told them they didn't understand life."

John Lennon*

---

* **John Winston Ono Lennon** MBE (born John Winston Lennon; 9 October 1940 – 8 December 1980) was an English singer and songwriter who rose to worldwide fame as a co-founder of the band the Beatles, the most commercially successful band in the history of popular music.

"Are we here to laugh or to cry?
Are we dying or being born?
Terra Nostra, Carlos Fuentes*

PREFACE TO THE INTERNATIONAL EDITION

A better world starts with you!

We the humans are in awe at how the world is swept by developments in the last two centuries and the digitalization from the 1980s on. Is this unexpected? Not exactly. **Alvin Toffler**, great futurologist, and a real scientist, in my opinion, stated in his trilogy he penned years ago, what was coming.

In his trilogy **Future Shock, Powershift, Third Wave**, Toffler talks about an uncertain and unbeknown future and us being drifted around as fearing and anxious creatures. Plus, there is a description of power. Does not he talk about the present in the intro section of his book Third Wave? Comments in parenthesis are mine.

"In a time when terrorists play death-games with hostages **(ISIS and hostages it has taken)**, as currencies careen amid rumors of a third World War **(Not only did currencies careen, WWIII actually started)**, as embassies flame **(almost every embassy in the**

---

* (From Alvin Toffler's preface for Third Wave) **Carlos Fuentes Macías** (November 11, 1928 – May 15, 2012) was a Mexican novelist and essayist.

Mediterranean region, as well as Africa and the Middle East, is under threat, and the Turkish Consulate in Mosul was raided and the officials there were held hostage for weeks)** and storm troopers lace up their boots in many lands, we stare in horror at the headlines **(multiply by five a number of fear people felt in the 90s)**. The price of gold—that sensitive barometer of fear—breaks all records **(true; an ounce even went as high as 1883 USD on September 11, 2011)**. Banks tremble **(The situation is much worse today; no matter how much money is printed and bank securities bought, banks continue to tremble)**. Inflation rages out of control. And the governments of the world are reduced to paralysis or imbecility."

Looking back, Toffler was right. Things went even worse, though.

As thinkers following the state of affairs in the economy and the world, we need to interpret and remark on the world in referring to an individual as well as social development.

My book **"Never Look Back! You're Not Going That Way!"** claims that despite the rising bigotry and radical movements, despite everything one has to stand up straight and add value to oneself. In this manner, I owe a lot to **Jiddu Krishnamurti**. He was a universal philosopher, not just an Indian thinker. His ideas, leading to an effect similar to the Butterfly Effect, are still around.

Just like Krishnamurti, I believe the individual is important. Therefore, I give priority to human beings in my seminars and my book. This book, in a sense, is a book on humanity. Although topics on individual and professional development prevail matters relevant to my country also appear in the book. This is normal! Had I been living in the US I would have talked about problems relevant to the US. So, would not it be a fresh breath of air to hear about Turkey and the Mediterranean region from a Turkish author?

The real professionals I talk about here are all locals. This is a conscious choice for the international edition. Two of these have achieved international success in the US and one has done so in Germany. What's more, to the best of my knowledge, this is the first time Coca Cola Chairman Muhtar Kent is set up as a model and system in a personal and social development book.

I could have included more local and international persons in addition to these five professionals. However, that would have damaged the original style as well as causing us to meander. In addition, I believe that these people need to be recognized globally.

Why Is It Important to Be a Real Professional?

Within the capitalist system, which increasingly gets difficult where people are more and more constrained, it has become much more significant to determine specialization systems and to form a high career structure in line with one's personality. In the last 20-30 years, bosses have preferred to work with easy-going personnel in the name of competition, whether in the US, England or South Africa. With this state of affairs in developed countries so think about the situation in developing countries. I am very convicted that we need to swim against the current in this specific instance. If life is getting more and more difficult every day, shouldn't we be smarter and have more clear and meaningful targets?

Obviously, most of the responsibility falls on the state, that organization humanity prides itself in having established but which is not worth much in general. This is a too broad topic to be dwelled on here.

Our choices change, life speeds up, but still, we have no peace! For a long time now we're used to having washing machines at home and even dishwashers. Many things are automated. Living alone is much easier and more widespread than 40 years ago. Soon we'll have self-driving, fully automated and electric cars. However, there is one thing I'm sure about, and that's we will not be **happy**. We'll still be pushed by the system.

So, everyone has improved her/himself, to excel at her/his job and let others know that she/he is good. Otherwise, if we trust in the future without meaningful targets we'll have a hard time.

Why the REAL POWER?

Toffler, as well as many great philosophers, have come up with definitions of power. We can accept many of these highly respectable definitions.

I have come up with a more general and sensible definition. Moreover, in a sense, it covers all others.

In defining power and what I call the real power I underline two factors: The real power consists of a combination of strategy (intellect, planning) and motivation. As I mentioned in the beginning of the relevant chapter, this idea of real power covers many factors such as the psychological, personal (skills), social, emotional, logical, spiritual and rational factors, combined to form motivational prowess and strategic intelligence.

Industry 4.0: End of Humanity or the Beginning?

Last but not the least I would like to talk about Industry 4.0. Is Industry 4.0 the end of humanity or the beginning? In the 21st century when the Internet reaches every corner and drones attack an airport (I hope it does not happen) and modern-day psychos obfuscate suicide bombers by attacking with unidentifiable unmanned aerial vehicles, will we and great Western corporations' intent on developing Industry 4.0 be able to pay indemnities of the unemployed? Will the issue of security be on the decrease or increase? How will firms buying their products sell their own goods and to whom? Will the buyers be real people? Or will robots be buying goods now?

What Do We Need?

We need a super-body that analyzes, talks about integrates into a plan all resources on the planet including human resources. This cannot be done by the UN or bodies associated with it, or the WTO, for that matter. These are all organizations of the last century, built after WWII, after wars of power. They have long completed their missions.

We will not be happier as each country tries to maximize its stakes. On the contrary, clashes will increase and destruction will ensue. As it is the system in general, as well as history, has benefited from destruction. Such armaments, such arms stocks will sooner or later bite us in the back!

Oh God, please save us the humans and nature in general!

I hope you derive information, ideas, and pleasure from the book...

With Love and Knowledge,
Alper KUL
İstanbul

PREFACE

Human Resources lies at the root of our problems.

Dear readers, upon reading the book you will be confused for this is an unusual book.

First of all, it is written as a dialogue... Second, it touches on many topics. So, I'll tell you what it is not and you'll figure out yourself what it is.

And then I'll tell you about the biggest problem the world faces.

What this book is merely not!?

It is not just a personal development book...

It is not just a social development book...

It is not just a book on career systems and development...

It is not just a book talking about **Muhtar Kent**, Chairman of Coca Cola for the first time...

It is not just a book on why **Professor Mehmet Öz (Dr. Oz)** is one the most professional and well-known doctor in the world...

It is not just a book telling who **Professor Onur Güntürkün** is for the first time...

It does not just contain unemployment numbers and analysis...

It is not just a book on global economy and developments...

It is not just a book on sectors on the rise...

It is not just a book on some hints to a successful business life...

It is not just a book on technique associated with shaping your resume...

It is not just a book that drags certain sectors in the mud...

It is not just a book on the Career Train...

It is not just a book on the lamentable state of being of the real economy...

It is not just a book on how to land a job or the fact that the hardest thing in life is finding a rewarding and pleasing job...

It is a book on **TRUTH...**

It is about **YOU...**

It is a book about hope, the intellect, love...

* * *

I have worked at many firms, and I have many friends and acquaintances working in the most important firms and institutions in the world.

The word around the campfire is "The management is problematic here!"

The truth is, although this statement is true it is incomplete and mistaken.

The basic issue of many countries including countries in the Middle East, Central Asia, and the Mediterranean, and even in the developed world, like US and others, has to do with **human resources**.

Please do not take the term "human resources" too technically in the literal sense. It has a wide and well-rounded coverage. We are not talking about the job two HR managers can dish up, but a much more special and deeper system and principle.

It is in this sense that the basic and most urgent issue of the whole world it is **Human Resources...**

We encounter problems related to human resources and resultant management issues wherever we go, including political parties, factories, schools, sports clubs and associations, universities, municipalities, civil non-governmental bodies, trade associations and agricultural cooperatives.

The essential matter here is the frenetic increase of population, and unplanned and unpredictable urbanization, and the ensuing chaos, depression, lack of empathy, and an unsound life.

It all has to do with love for humanity and focus on quality, with actually implementing intellect and science, with having prudence and a long-term look at events.

We are in dire need of leaders and systems that will bring forth quality for it is a quality that breeds the correct human resource.

An approach focused on profits and profits only has crashed in Eastern Mediterranean countries as well as big countries such as the US. As the eminent writer Amin Maalouf has stated, the world has entered the new century without a compass.

In the book, I aim to tackle issues with a 360° approach. I apologize in advance for any failures and mistakes. Mistakes, material and otherwise, shall certainly come to light in later editions and be corrected.

Were it not for **Ayşe Özbay Erozan**, my translator and whom I believe is one of the most professional translators of our country, I would not have reached out to you in English of such high-quality. For this, I thank her very much.

I wish you a pleasant business life where you can become a real professional and a life is superb as the five-wings windmill.

Alper KUL
Istanbul

"Scio me nihil scire."
"All I know is that I know nothing."

Socrates*

---

*   Socrates (470/469 – 399 BC) was a classical Greek (Athenian) philosopher credited as one of the founders of Western philosophy. He is an enigmatic figure known chiefly through the accounts of classical writers, especially the writings of his students Plato and Xenophon and the plays of his contemporary Aristophanes.

1

MODEL OF WINDMILL WITH 5 WINGS

– **Mr. Career, why are you called that?**
– A few years ago, I went to Cyprus to give talks. There were five people one of whom was Mr. Expression. In following encounters Mr. Expression, probably impressed by my thoughts on business life in general, suggested that I use the pseudonym Mr. Business. It seemed reasonable at first, but when I reconsidered it, bearing in mind my sensitivity for mother tongue, I thought Mr. Career would be better. I've been giving talks and seminars using this pseudonym, which I especially emphasized in 2010-12. Actually, I've been giving talks since 2007 on career and self-improvement.

– **So why did you prefer to talk to me?**
– Well, the easiest and best way to reach out to the audience is through dialogues. Platon, in his Socrates' Apology as well as other works he's employed this method. Plus, other philosophers employ this method to convey difficult and complex ideas.

– **So, the fact that we are having this conversation is because career development and business life are as difficult as philosophical issues?**
– As a matter fact, I'd love to have Socrates, born in Alopecia in 469 BC, and Plato, a disciple of the former and a great thinker, here with us. They could have made insightful comments... For

instance, in his apology, Plato reiterates Chaerephon, Socrates' friend who went to the sanctuary of Delphi, regarding Pythia the Oracle. Chaerephon asks Pythia if there is a man on earth wiser than Socrates, upon which she says that there is not. Socrates, being the wise man, he is, is in doubt because he knows that what he knows is nothing. But he is not to doubt the words of the oracle since gods would not lie. Thus, taking the Oracle's words as a puzzle, he starts to search. First, he goes to the politician, then to poets, then to masters and artisans known for their wisdom (Sophia). Through questions, he poses he knows that they are not wise but wallow in ignorance. They think they know what in fact they do not know; in addition, they do not know what they do not know. Ignorance is the worst of all evils. In contrast, Socrates knows that he does not know, which makes him wiser than these people. Socrates displays the human wisdom of being aware of one's ignorance. Socrates knows himself. Our business or private lives may have simple statements just as philosophy does. Still, I think we know little and there are many places for learning and improvement. I think the most important issue on our agenda should be **"career philosophy"** because we spend the most significant and nicest part of our lives working.

– **So, is knowing oneself of utmost importance?**
– Precisely, in both arenas knowing oneself is the most important matter. A person who knows herself causes no harm and is crystal clear. She is happy.

– **How does one get to know oneself?**
– Easy. There is training for that. I attended a two-day seminar on "self-managing leadership" at my alma mater, **Koç University**. This was nine years after I graduated. Truth be told, this two-day seminar was way more effective than five years' worth of education! It was highly efficient, beneficial and filled with "philosophy". At the end of this seminar, you make a drawing like a mind map and express your life goal through various forms and symbols.

– **Well, may I ask what you drew?**
– I made a drawing of happiness or a satisfactory life.

– **Is that so!**
– Yep, I remember clearly. I drew a windmill. If wind power is life energy and our God-given power, there should be five wings to the windmill. If these wings are construed and fitted correctly the operation will be optimized. On the other hand, if one of the wings is missing the mill will lose power. One aspect of knowing yourself is being by yourself and defining your ideas. I will dwell to this later.

– **So, your contention is that wings are all that matters...**
– Not only the wings, of course. The size of the mill, materials it's made of, its sturdiness, agents of power transfer, and most important of all, how you channel the outcoming power, all matter.

– **OK, so, this conversation shall turn into a book. Will you mention the five wings or is it going to be primarily about career development?**
– As I said before if you know yourself and develop the five wings in a suitable fashion you could have a very satisfactory life. Business is, of course, one of these five wings. From time to time we need to call this the career wing. In fact, the two are not the same. Not everyone who works is pursuing a career. The other four are separate from a career. Let's go into some detail: The second wing I'd like to call **sport** (athletic life). Sports is a critical factor in a person's life because doing sports clears one's mind and your flow of ideas increases. In short, physical strength is what makes you strong. This wing, although quite overlooked in most societies, is highly significant. Another wing is the **intellect.** Intellectual capacity is the most distinguishing capacity. The way to this is reading a lot. But the most important factor is comprehending what you read.

– **So, the difference between an intellectual and someone who reads a lot lies where?**

– Simple. Intellectual reads very different books. He does not limit himself to one area. He delves into as many areas as he can. We need to look more into the word itself. Do you know who an intellectual is?

– **An enlightened person...**
– No "enlightened" is a very special word and not everyone can be an enlightened person. It is full of meaning and power. "Intellectual" as a word, has roots in the Latin word "intellectus". It is rumination, understanding, trying to understand reasons behind the façade and being a profound human being. To be frank everyone, from the simple Simon to the top-level executive, can be an intellectual.

An intellectual is someone who thinks.

– **Cogito ergo sum, is it?**
– Exactly, if you think you exist. This is more so in business.

- What if everyone thinks and wants to go into business to become an exec?
- The dictionary definition of an intellectual is someone use puts to use her intellect and ability to think analytically for her occupational or to advance personal aims. So, in that sense, everyone should use her intellect in the most correct and severest manner for occupational ends. But unfortunately, not everyone can be a **leader-manager** in the real sense of the word.

- Do you think being a leader is an inborn ability?
- Frankly, leadership is a very exceptional matter. Thousands of people have been racking their brains. The main topic here is not leadership but it is a significant issue in business. If you like I can talk about my experiences later.

- Ok then, later we'll do that. So, what do we need to do to develop our intellect, or as you'd like to call it, the intellectual wing of the windmill?
- Another wing is the **social wing**. This is as critical a wing as sports, career, and intellect. That is, it is a sine qua non. You know who is sociable?

    A sociable person is someone who is able to establish functional, correct, to-the-point, long-lasting relationships that make her happy.

    I call this **"social intelligence"**. It is defined among different types of intelligence. Later on, when I talk about intricacies of professional work I'll mention three basic facts. And of course, social intelligence ranks among these three factors.

- That makes four wings, can't wait to find out the last one!
- The **artistic wing** helps the creative side of a person come forward.
    Art is the most complementary factor that refines a person.

    What distinguishes a person with a high EQ from other is the amount of time she spares for arts and artistic activities. There is a definite connection between the intellectual wing and the artistic wing. However, being an intellectual does not necessarily entail caring about arts. It instills a proclivity.

You should try to draw a picture or play a musical instrument if you want to happy and lead a satisfying life. Percussion instruments, in particular, have a therapeutic and meditative quality to them. Unless they do it the wrong way, people who work with music do not ever need another method of meditation or therapy. And this also goes for drama and painting.

– **But not everyone can go into arts...**
– Everyone can busy themselves with arts...In my opinion, many things in life have an artistic quality to them. For instance, cooking well is an art. If you have no artistic interests, cook; at least you won't go hungry. I want to say more on this topic. Many people are under stress because of work. I must mention meditation.

To put it bluntly, either you meditate, which is not easy in the sense that you have to find a quiet and special spot, or you'll go into arts.

Relax, no one will blame you for making cacophonous sounds. People engaged in artistic activities are respected by others as long as they are not physically disturbed. Painting, charcoal drawings, even knitting is an artistic endeavor. Gardening is immensely fulfilling, and every gardener is an artist.

"The length of the unfolded wings cannot be known."

Andre Gide*

---

* André Paul Guillaume Gide (22 November 1869 – 19 February 1951) was a French author and winner of the Nobel Prize in Literature in 1947 "for his comprehensive and artistically significant writings, in which human problems and conditions have been presented with a fearless love of truth and keen psychological insight". Gide's career ranged from its beginnings in the symbolist movement, to the advent of anticolonialism between the two World Wars.

– **I still have some concerns over financial means. How will happen all these 5 wings?**
– As I said before this mill will not work with water. It will work with the wind. It will be made to evaluate the wind in a correct way. Taking the windmill as our prop, it is there to benefit from the wind. The source of the wind is the root of the **real power**, which I will talk about later. If the wind blows fiercely but your mill is limited in action. What then? Here come the well-designed and well-coordinated five wings.

Now granted, it's not easy to come up with such a carefully balanced mill. As Mr. Career and a person devoted to change the society in a positive manner, I have a duty to present basic philosophy. Plus, I don't think this is difficult and it is the essential fact of being a civilized person.

Really, why do we want to have careers? Any thoughts?

– **For money...**
– Wrong. There are simpler and faster ways.

– **For a coordinated life...**
– Wrong again...

You can achieve an orderly life by farming or just by gardening. If you have a normal job and a good family, you have an orderly life.

The word "Career" passed from French to all languages. *"Carrière"* is a geographical term. It means "a road that goes somewhere; a road that comes". The word in and of itself refers to the path hikers (those who walk on mountain trails) take...

To have a career means the path that you take is an adventure.

When you look at it this way, it's like walking into the unknown. Different from other standard professions and jobs, people who what to have a career are actually saying this: *"I'm on a path and I'm moving forward...I have a goal. My goal is to reach the peaks over there. I will listen to and spend time with whoever helps me on to my goal and brings me along the shortest and safest path."*

Or I could explain it like this:

"In the end, I'm going to reach my goal. This means the important thing is that while traveling this path, I gain experience and it's a satisfying journey. In a sense, everyone may not reach the top, especially since only a few people can reach the summit."

The actual goal is to receive enjoyment and pleasure from the journey, it's how equipped you are. In every career description, we come across this: *"From the perspective of the profession, elevation of professional qualities. Or from an academic perspective, elevation of class in varying different degrees and tiers..."*

As you can see, there's always a look toward goals and growth.

– **I understand.**
– **Aziz Nesin*** summarized well what I want to explain...

"Your work is going to be hard. Always try the difficult. Even if you can't do the difficult, while trying to do the difficult, you are accomplishing the easy."

– **Where is this world heading?**
– Have you ever read the book, **Disordered World** by Amin Maalouf? It's interesting, in 2009 Amin Maalouf sensed the coming uprising in North Africa and in the Middle East that happened and are still going on. That is to say, those who read Maalouf's great book were not surprised when the "Jasmine Revolution" in Tunisia and the events in Egypt, Libya, Bahrain,

---

* Aziz Nesin (born Mehmet Nusret Nesin, December 20, 1915 – July 6, 1995) was a Turkish writer and humorist who authored more than 100 books.

Jordan, and Algeria took place. And in the end Syria. But Syria rests on a different and special reason, but the departure point is the same, or let's say international powers' exploitation:

Youth unemployment.

Today the greatest problem in the world is youth unemployment. In the coming ten years and in fact for a longer period of time, it will make its mark. Amin Maalouf mentions youth unemployment but not as the only reason. However, like I've said for years: **youth unemployment is our region's greatest problem.**

– **Did Maalouf see the future?**
– No, there's no need to see the future. Maalouf is a writer and thinker who lives in France. He follows closely the events with the Arabs and the Middle East. He's been to Turkey many times and the books he's written have had a strong impact. He knows **Atatürk** quite well and has analyzed the effects **Atatürk** has had on Arab society.

Of course, Maalouf doesn't say in his book that the uprising will happen, but he analyzes well the reasons the Arab world is behind and why it hasn't been able to escape the vicious circle it's in.

– **I'm definitely going to read this book. So, what do you think is the reason for all these events? Is the world going down?**
– Because my profession is in international marketing and sales, I have to follow what's going on in the world. Have you ever heard the word *"Hittiste"*?

– **Is it French?**
– Yes, you're close. *Hittiste* is a word that is used in French-Arabic and means "urban poor". The unemployed youth of Tunisia are referred to as *"Hittiste"*.

How much more there are...for example, what does *Shabab Atileen* mean? The unemployed youth of Egypt are called *Shabab Atileen*. There were many reasons for the events in Egypt, but one of them is the *Shababs* who are without hope. Amin Maalouf came to my mind again. He, when describing the world in the 21. century, likened it to a ship without a compass. Or to use my description, a mountain climber without a guide. He's absolutely right. In 2009, he was asserting that the ship without the compass is at a loss as to what to do before the storm but when the storm comes — and I think it came — it is in for total destruction. This is quite true. We are headed for a big catastrophe.

– **What about the other regions?**
– Are you assuming that the *Hittistes* and the *Shababs* are alone?

In England, they refer to them as *Neet,* youth who are uneducated and unemployed or without enough experience. They even have a name for them in Japan: *Freeteer*. It comes from the English *freelance* and the German *Arbeiter* (worker).

The Spanish gave the name *Mileurista* to this segment of society. In Spanish, "Mille" means "a thousand". So, it means in one month they are earning less than 1000 Euro or maximum 1000 Euro.

In America, these young people are referred to as *Boomerang*. What is a boomerang? It's a tool that is made by Aboriginal Australians. When you throw it in the air it goes and returns to you. In this sense, Americans mean this: These youths spend thousands of dollars on American universities only to return home due to not finding work. Just like a boomerang...

– **So, is there a problem with large, rising economies like China?**
– How could there not? In addition, there are levels. In the last 10 years China has grown 10 percent every year but so has the population. In China, there are *"Ant Tribes"*.

– **What does this mean?**
– Bloomberg Businessweek explained it like this:

> *"Youth who have graduated from university but have not found a job with a good income and are sharing a cheap apartment with others are referred to as an 'Ant Tribe'."*

Only in developing countries have the problems not been seen. Today, from Greece to Italy and France, and from there to

England, and even as far as the United States, there are serious problems. As well, the rebellions are not just in North Africa.

You know that in 2012 the youth of Greece the really stirred up trouble. Today Greece is experiencing nothing like it ever has in its history. Unlike Germany or Austria, Greece doesn't have the enough economic resources, the chance of Greece's recovery is minimal. Concrete statistics aren't needed at all. Life and what has happened is clearly out in the open.

Further, numbers can't explain exactly what the people have experienced. On the contrary, they mask what the people have lived through and the hardships they have suffered.

– **What do you think is the factor that set off these events?**
– It's very simple. In the setting of the 2008 - 2009 economic crisis, all the balances were turned over and the system was shaken to the core. The result is crises that are unending and don't want to end.

– **How is that?**
– It's like this, the latest economic crisis caused the decline in European and American tourists. This is because everyone needed to act more conservatively and spend less money. After all, some remained unemployed. This prevented them from traveling abroad. So, who is affected most by this situation? Of course, countries like Tunisia and Greece are affected, as well as Egypt.

The truth is that the problems cannot be explained simply by the tourism situation, but whatever happened, tourism is at a standstill. I am corresponding with and talking to my Greek friends. One of my friends who is a manager at a high-class hotel in the center of Athens is saying that the situation is getting worse because tourists are not coming; as a former resident of Istanbul, he would like to return to Turkey. Hearing this really affected me. I was thinking on this topic...in Tunisia, rebellions happened. When you look at their economy, it's no surprise. Their economy is based heavily on tourism and is completely dependent on the outside.

So, this sort of spiral effect is emerging. Therefore, it's not overly pretentious to say that the United States of America's worsening economy and mortgage crisis paved the way for the "Jasmine Rebellion".

– **Don't you think this is an overly assertive analysis?**
– I think the exact opposite. It's a very clear analysis. It had been said that America's poor management had the ability to affect everyone and that's what happened.

Actually, writers who possess foresight such as Maalouf or economist and Nobel Prize winner, Paul Krugman, said the results would be global. I'm just laying out the situation a bit more. Of course, I know quite well the political and strategic reasons. But without an economic basis, it's difficult to get results through political pressures or manipulations. First, the people must feel the pressure.

My concern is the future of youth as well as the wider spectrum of people. In this sense, we must understand the world better. Otherwise, we would have started talking about Turkey's problems right away. The United Kingdom's Minister of State for Employment, Chris Grayling (later the Secretary of State for Justice), likened *chronic unemployment to a timed bomb about ready to explode.* In the Bloomberg Businessweek magazine that I'm holding, Jeffrey Joerres, the CEO of Manpower (a world-renowned human resource firm), makes the statement,

> "It's clear that if we don't take steps, in the next year youth unemployment will be the epidemic of this decade. You can't afford to ignore the issue."

I think that this statement by Mr. Joerres is more important than the speeches of all the government officials. Despite the fact that I have sharply criticized **"head hunter"** firms and the like, they have a specialty that is very important. They keep a pulse on work world and understand the state of affairs better than many politicians and heads of state.

– **Isn't there an economic crisis every four years? In fact, isn't there a big crisis every ten years? Why these new events now?**

– That's a great question. Yes, that's exactly it. Every 4-5 years we experience a financial crisis. It was predicted that the drought crisis in America in the summer of 2012 would bring on an agricultural crisis.

Now the word **"crisis"** has lost its meaning. Pardon me, but they caused the word to become useless! Every event or drought that has resulted in a supply problem has been called a "crisis". A crisis doesn't arise this easily. The effects of crises are global, and very seriously damaging consequences occur. The crises that happen every 5 years are not actually crises in the true sense of the word. You can call them ripples as in the financial world.

In America when the soy bean and wheat production numbers fall, from around here it is said, "Oh no, bread prices are going to rise." This is a big neglect and speculation. It's too bad since Turkey is a strong producer of wheat. Just the opposite, these types of comments should be made, "We wish that our watering systems were much more developed!" and "Right now we wish that we had extra wheat to export to America!"

We don't say those things. We say, "Oh no, we're in trouble! The bread prices are going to rise!" Or let's say that we did not have a drought but had extra produce, at how high of price could we have exported? How can we increase our agricultural input? We're not debating these things.

– **So, are those who are saying these things wrong? We're talking about a 50-year drought... Is there not a drought in country? Has it not been experienced?**

– I'm not denying the problem with statistics and numbers, but one must be careful. Further, there are already big problems in agriculture. Should a drought come?

There are some saying that if we continue at the current population increase, ten years later we will go hungry. We must listen and seek to understand these things.

I was going to give you wheat production numbers, but I decided against making bothering you with numbers. I just want to say this, drought isn't the only factor affecting wheat prices. Another basic factor is grains used as "bio-fuel".

Listen to what the Union of Chambers of Agriculture General Secretary, Şemsi Bayraktar has to say:

> "On the other hand, according to the findings of several international organizations, fears that fossil fuels will decrease and high energy costs have caused interest in biofuels to increase. Another factor is that the result of using grains like wheat and corn as well as plant-based oils such as canola, soybean sunflower to produce biofuels will result in a rise in usage prices to be able to produce the needed the energy for wheat as a food product to be consumed. With wheat, the rising world population, rise in incomes, food safety and changing consumer habits also cause the rise in prices."

As Şemsi Bayraktar appropriately said, there are many factors that cause the rise in prices. What I wanted to explain is that this isn't the first-time drought has happened and it won't be the last... In fact, suppose that in America after discovering shale gas and China's reduction in the consumption of petroleum, the price of fossil fuels drops and the supply problem becomes irrelevant. Then the demand for biofuels would drop and the prices for wheat and grains would become stabilized, etc.

My concern is this: the figures as hypothesized are not unbelievably terrible. But if you read the magazines, we've been burned, used up and finished. So, the soybean prices of 2008 caused the insurrections in over 30 countries. And the news continues in this way: *"It is feared that the sharp rise in food prices could pave the way for new social upheavals and political crises."*

However, the same news is also saying that the wheat prices have not reached the levels of 2008. In other words, the prices in 2008 were higher. When we look at it, the most important factor is the population increase but without the increase in world food stocks. Biofuel usage...

But who is responsible for this? Mother Nature who keeps on giving? But isn't it humans who are continually and excessively reproducing themselves?

The fundamental reason for the lack of world food stocks and **youth unemployment** is a **wild increase in population.** Large and long-lasting wars aren't breaking out anymore and widespread epidemic diseases aren't appearing. The lifespan of the human being lengthened, this is due to great advances in the medical and pharmaceutical industries.

> "Because learning does not consist only of knowing what we must or we can do, but also of knowing what we could do and perhaps should not do."
>
> Umberto Eco*

---

* Umberto Eco OMRI (5 January 1932 – 19 February 2016) was an Italian novelist, literary critic, philosopher, semiotician, and university professor. He is best known internationally for his 1980 novel Il nome della rosa (The Name of the Rose), a historical mystery combining semiotics in fiction with biblical analysis, medieval studies, and literary theory. He later wrote other novels, including Il pendolo di Foucault (Foucault's Pendulum) and L'isola del giorno prima (The Island of the Day Before). His novel Il cimitero di Praga (The Prague Cemetery), released in 2010, topped the bestseller charts in Italy. Eco also wrote academic texts, children's books, and essays. He was the founder of the Department of media studies at the University of the Republic of San Marino, president of the Graduate School for the Study of the Humanities at the University of Bologna, member of the Accademia dei Lincei, and an honorary fellow of Kellogg College, Oxford. (Source: Wikipedia)

– **In this situation, every person has the ability to work more!**
– That's exactly it. Can you imagine? In the past, to turn 60 years old meant that everything was taken from under you and you left the workforce. Now, forget 60 years. We're currently in a period where leaving the workforce almost means that a second career can begin. People after this age are doing consulting or they are taking new hobbies. They are continuing to develop themselves. There's a trend called **"Transhumanism"**. Have you heard of it?

– **No, I haven't heard of it.**
– Transhumans are those who work to extend the lives of humans. This intensely serious group is not only working in the field of physics and science but at the same time also researching the philosophical and emotional dimensions. Those working in top universities In England and other developed countries are receiving criticism.

What I want to say is this, there is transhumanism in one hand, stem cell research in another, and modern medicine as well as the media system promoting health and long life. When we consider all of these, long life is now an essential and something to which modern man has earned the right. Another assertion is that we definitely need to produce fewer children. One child would be the ideal. Of course, we could support the idea that those who have the means could produce more children. **However, they truly must have plenty of means.**

– **If we return to the topic of crises...**
– In today's world, there are huge disagreements between finance capitalists and those in the real sector, that is those powers who

primarily rely on industry. The banks are the largest agents in finance capitalism. There are many agents in the real sector. It's impossible to count, but the information industry (IT industry) has been added to all of them. **At this stage, there are three sides in the war.**

– **So, you are saying that there is a three-way seizing war going on in the world. So, is this the cause of the crises?**
– Yes, the crises are due competition among the powers. In today's world, companies have become so large and strong that governments are dwarfed next to them. This is an interesting situation. Which one do we mention? For example, Samsung is an amazing firm. It's as if there is no sector they aren't involved in. They produce everything from the smallest telephone to televisions, from trucks to space satellites, and from washing machines to music systems.

Of all the firms, Apple is mostly hesitating of Samsung. In this light, it's a source of pride for the little country called South Korea to go up against Great America.

– **Why?**
– Oh, South Korea, with Samsung and Hyundai, they are standing up the world. Today the telephones that challenge the iPhone the most are produced by Samsung. In southeast Asia, they have a huge part of the market, and while the iPhone doesn't put out a new phone for a while, Samsung catches up and, in fact, surpasses them in sales. Whenever iPhone puts a new version out on the market, that is when sales increase.

This is what I'm trying to say, in today's world, the industries rooted in information and technology have passed the classic industries.

When you look at the world's largest firms, among them there are not many producers of electronics. The majority are oil companies. Because in a world that runs under political protection and naturally increasing energy needs, oil companies naturally have a lot of turnovers. Oil companies are completely dependent on political systems, but those companies that produce electronic and what we call hi-tech products have no need for political protection.

No matter what products they produce, they cross political borders and enter in; If you don't want to fall behind, in one way or another those products must be integrated into your system and be submitted to the market. Information and technology firms, if not always, most of the times they are successful. Because of this, they don't have the need for high political support. One or two smart designed incentives can help them dramatically.

For, their share capital is not the black gold that is mentioned to us by the god. Their funds are one. That is intelligence.

At this point, I want to ask you something. For example, take Apple or Samsung, Oracle, and SAP. While software companies like these are doing their amazingly genius work, what did the banks do? The fundamental reason for the latest crises and the states of Europe is the banks. Now everyone knows this is and is articulating it. In the last 20 years, the stock markets, banks, and the topsy-turvy markets have been behind nearly every crisis.

Everyone knows that the mechanism called the market doesn't actually have anything to do with the general public, but no-one knows whether or not it has any real purpose.

Not so long ago in the summer months of 2012, tourism giant Spain was being called superb and star of the future. Nearly every day it put on a good show. Its situation was actually beyond the grave... In Spain, the unemployment rate is near 26 percent; 6 million people are looking for work, and the people are very distressed. The Spanish banks haven't had their fill of money. The increase in requests for assistance has bombarded the government and the government squeezing the European Union.

As you can tell the tire went flat, and the vehicle is heading toward a cliff. It falls on the mayor of the Andalusian town of **Marinaleda, Juan Manuel Sánchez Gordillo** to say that the king has no clothes on. A newspaper in 2012 wrote something like this:

"In the first place, Juan Manuel Sánchez Gordillo, who started a march in his region that continued for three weeks, has made a name for himself participating with the union presidents in protest marches. Later, in order to incite civil rebellion, the neighboring governors of the group started a three-week march."

The article continues: *"Taking on the name "Robin Hood", Juan Manuel Sánchez Gordillo turned his eyes to the banks. Gordillo, saying they were fighting against poverty, said that all the banks and markets would be overrun."*

Here he also said something else very interesting: *"It's obvious that while the bankers send the money that they had robbed from their customers to tax to havens, also the political parties are corrupted too."*

The most interesting thing is this: *"Due to hunger, in the invasions that happened, the information released was that only the most needed milk, sugar, olive oil, and rice were taken."*

– **And in an olive oil country!**
– Exactly. How interesting, isn't it? This results from poor governance and the European Union's faulty control mechanisms. If the European Union recovers from this turbulence, they will have established an unbelievable central control system. All of these faulty systems brought the European Union to the brink of dispersion. If we don't understand the mechanisms that pave the way to crisis and crises one after another, then we can't understand our problems (all over the World unemployment crisis), and most likely, we will just watch unemployment rise.

* * *

"We have forty million reasons for failure, but not a single excuse."

Rudyard Kipling

* * *

– I'd like to come to move on to the rebellions and the latest events in Syria. Are there political and economic reasons? And what role do you think the great powers play?

– When I analyze events, I find it more appropriate to analyze from the perspective of the roles of the political and international organizations and the governments. Because this type of analysis is enjoyable and you can easily bring into question many countries and their stability. Furthermore, this approach is open to conspiracy theories. Yes, it's true that in this oil region the international balances and rivalry are the most important factors. Actually, this shouldn't be forgotten. If there weren't youth unemployment, these outside powers wouldn't have a place to take shelter. I'm not saying that youth unemployment is the root of everything, but it is the most important reason.

Today the event that is called "Arab Spring" is the rebellion of unemployed youth and those without a shred of hope in life. Behind the events in Syria, there is a political tussle between Russia and America.

Everyone has powers that support them. It's a like the pacts that were in place during the world wars. **In this light, this civil war is World War III.** But no one is brave enough to call it that!

– **So, will these rebellions bring about a good future?**
– I would have loved to interview Amin Maalouf on this point. I assume not...

We remember that in 2012 bad news from Tunisia began to come in about women's rights. The situation is looking critical. "Great" news isn't coming from Egypt too. In the April 2013 issue of the **"21st Century"** magazine, a very detailed interview with the Egyptian ambassador to Turkey, the esteemed Abderahman Salaheldin, was published. Here I want to share with you what the magazine's editors highlighted with red letters.

> *"The rebellion is waiting for two goals to be accomplished. This is, in reality, a test of the government. If the work and social justice department are able to provide solutions, then they will be successful and will be reelected. However, if they aren't suc-*

cessful, they will not be reelected. We are all agreed on one matter. The change will happen with peace and democracy, not with the use of force and violence."

You know that a short time later after saying these words, "Mursi" was overthrown. And in his place, a provisional government was put in place... Will change come with peace or with democracy? Or will it happen? I don't really want to enter the political side of work since our problems are youth unemployment, general unemployment, and beyond that hopelessness. Actually, when looking at career life and work life, the foundational emotion we need to have is this: **a world of hope**...

– **Is there no hope in the Arab world or the Middle East?**
– I don't think there is. Because about these some of the countries, including Turkey, we can say this: In these countries, there is a serious problem with feeling **hopeless**. These countries aren't even last in the line of capitalist and democratic systems. When talking about Turkey we can look even closer. But I want to talk more about the words "hope" and "hopelessness". Because the faulty functioning of the economic systems delivers people over to this feeling of **hopelessness**. In the world, there are two dangerous feelings, **hopelessness and worry**. These two feelings scare you. In this manner, a third feeling surfaces: **fear**.

We experience these fears a lot in our career lives. Every young person in the spring of his career experiences these feelings. In fact, even in advanced stages of the career ladder, these feelings can seize you. Even when retiring, you have concerns.

We know this from our elders. The level of worry that one has who fears he may lose his high-paying job is different from the youth who has nothing to lose. Even so, they experience similar feelings.

Years ago, I read a book: **The World of Hope** by Şevket Rado*.

Şevket Rado was saying this: *"This world is neither this world nor that world, it is the world of hope. Hope."*

---

* Şevket Rado (1913-1988). He was one of the most compelling poet, journalist, radio producer, teacher, business man and writer in Turkey.

From a book that I read twenty years ago, these words have stayed with me the most. That's really the way it is. I completely agree with Şevket Rado. Hopelessness is very dangerous. If you leave people a long time without hope, all of your other principles and social systems could cave in.

Today, the traditional capitalist system leads us to think of a certain template. In this template, the factor that there are some who think quite differently and are creative is disregarded. In essence, career life in this expression is very complicated. Yet, sadly I must say that for people who are **creative** and **developers** sometimes their career paths may be boring and lacking.

Sometime in the future while doing sector and vocational evaluations, I will have more points to make on this topic. Also, at the end of our conversation, I'm going to explain to you the basic model of Turkish work life. Actually, this isn't just our problem, it's worldwide. It's universal.

– **Considering this, could we move from the Arab world to our country?**
– Of course, my goal is to better analyze those who surround Turkey. Everyone and every country are affected by the "habitat" in which they are found. Turkey in this sense cannot be considered lucky, however also is not in all that terrible of a situation. I believe that despite the problems of our neighbors and other problems, Turkey is better than its neighbors. This country's core and the foundation are strong.

However, Turkey is still not able to emancipate itself from its problems. So, all of these open the way for us to enter a severe **"hopeless"** vortex and squeezing the society.

– **Are the Turkish people hopeless? And if I could ask you personally, are you hopeless?**
– No, I'm not hopeless. However, we've lost a lot of blood, and components in both our work lives and social systems have broken down and have worn out. But I think the people are hopeless. And worse, they don't know how they are going to break out of feeling that way. Business life is also not going well.

– **Don't you think your comments are severe?**
– This is not commentary. It's reality. If you want, we can start by analyzing the unemployment numbers. Especially as one who frequently goes to Europe, I can see the gravity of the situation quite clearly.

– **Of what sort? You had mentioned there was a crisis in Europe.**
– Precisely. That's why it's grave. It could be said that this period is a time in which Turkey has the most potential for the accelerated rise, the youth, and unbelievable potential could be utilized, and this potential could be turned into a flood of hope with extraordinary growth.

It's true that Europe's situation is bad. However, Turkey in many aspects is a worse and more hopeless circumstance. The reason is as follows. The development of Europe has completed; at this point, it's grown old; and may be the youth population is comparatively weak. But there's a difference. The youth over there don't have huge challenges. There's unemployment, but there's also insurance for unemployment. When you look at it, only because of this there are people not working.

This is government politics. European countries are not able to create employment opportunities for these youths. So, at the very least, they work to prevent them from going hungry. In this way, they try to not create social problems.

Before, I mentioned the youth of Greece and England. Some countries like Germany are experiencing only a minor unemployment problem and their infrastructure is very strong. In a sense, there's not one Europe. There are very different "European countries and regions".

Where you have lived is important. I find it more correct to compare Turkey to Germany rather than to Italy as everyone loves to do. That way, there will be comparison points so that you can compare yourself to the country that has the best system and the best way of governing.

– **But the two cultures are so different...**
– I know that the cultures are different, but it's not just about the only culture. Culture is engine power. So, called universal cul-

ture is a type of culture, and **universal culture** is not a value that belongs to just one nation. Universal culture is like a virus. If you directly inject people with the virus, you will obtain proper and contemporary values.

If you compare Middle Age and New Age Italian governments with German principalities, you see that they are a far from one another. In that period, the Germans were very behind culturally, economically, and socially. Furthermore, if we go back much further, the fathers of the Germans, the Teutons (Latin: Teutones), were viewed by the Romans as being the most savage of all the barbarian clans. The difference at that time is too much to even be compared.

The Mediterranean basin has always been superior, and today, the cultural development that we call Western civilization was fashioned in the Mediterranean basin.

Actually, not only the Germans but the northern societies, in general, went on the attack in the 19th century. This is due to the fact that they were hard pressed as a result of attacks by France and England in the west and the Austro-Hungarian Empire in the south and the Russian attacks from the East. In particular, Finland suffered much under Russian rule. All of these countries, especially Finland, are examples of putting forth incredible campaigns.

Even though these countries made huge mistakes, they reached their desired goals in the 20th century. They entered the 20th and 21st centuries quite well. They raised their youth well. They injected themselves with the values of universal culture, and groundbreaking ideas of western civilization passed on to these countries.

Italy, of course, is always Italy. The Italians for the last 30, maybe 50 years have managed the country very poorly. There were serious mafia problems, and in recent years, the central government became very weak. Concerning this last crisis, the same thing can be said for Spain. If you look at their loan interest rates, you will better see what I mean.

Of course, interest rates only won't explain the gap. Today, the problem in nearly every country in the Mediterranean Basin is chronic unemployment: Italy, Spain, Greece, Tunisia, Egypt, Turkey, France, Algeria, Slovenia, Albania, Croatia, Macedonia, Bosnia Herzegovina, Nagorno-Karabakh, Israel, Lebanon, Morocco, Palestine, Libya, Portugal (even though it's not really Mediterranean, it's a part of its culture), and Syria. The ancient world's most splendid countries and regions, which had been the founders of the Renaissance and the Enlightenment Age, are now wrestling with huge problems. Among these, Turkey was being described as a shining star! You figure out the rest.

– I understand.
– If you want to see development and system, you need to take a look at Switzerland, Germany, Denmark, Holland, Finland, Sweden, Norway, Canada, Australia, Japan (possesses some problems that seem to be fading), South Korea, the United States, Hong Kong (fiscal system and liberal organizations), and Singapore.

So, do these countries that I have listed have no problems? Of course, there are, but there's one difference. **They give high importance to the real development of the human and to what's called the Human Development Index level.** Except for the United States, chronic unemployment is not a problem in these countries (Unemployment in the United States in 2017 fell below 5 percent). These are countries that have a reasonable amount of unemployment and yet some of these countries still have a high rate of immigration.

To allow immigration is not a bad thing. This actually shows that that the urban centers and regions of that country truly have become desirable hubs and in order to develop and there is a need for human resources who can take on the second-class jobs. Furthermore, countries such as Canada are very meticulous in their immigration policies. The standard for their incoming immigrants is high.

Canada has opened their doors to not only English and French speaking immigrants but also those who have a different mother tongue. **Actually, if they were to develop a little more encour-**

aging politics, it would be possible for them to pull more quality immigrants from the Mediterranean region.

Also, if you go to the southward, there's the reality of Africa. Africa has past and present colonization. We say, "poor Africa", but, from my perspective, the situation of those in the Mediterranean Basin, us included, is not that bright.

– **In this situation, you are saying that, in comparison to these countries, there's no chance for Turkey to stay behind and be caught.**
– No, that's not what I'm saying. Maybe you will suppose that I'm thinking quite positively, but first I do evaluate the current situation. So now what I'm saying is that whether it's from the perspective of government productivity or the structuring of the private sector, our situation is not good. However, this is not something that cannot be solved. We are surrounded by examples. For example, South Korea or the old Northern European countries as I described them. Or in the distant past, again Russia and again old Japan. There are many examples of those who have taken off.

– **Didn't take off during Turgut Özal's time?**
– That was different. That was an expansion. We passed from a closed economy to an open one. We placed ourselves on the launching pad. However, except for the first years of the Republic, I have not seen or heard any who has truly launched the country and given the youth and people of this country hope.

– **But they are saying that in the last ten years we have gone on the attack.**
– I'd like to have a conversation about career and personal development. If we keep looking at the general situation of our country and evaluate every period, we will be far removed from our topic. Of course, the beginning of everything is good administration. If you can't have good administration, you will be face to face with, as they say in English "mismanagement", that is "faulty and lacking management".

We are passing through these days where the Human Development Index in Turkey is not improving largely because our country is heavily dependent on construction and related sectors and to some degree the automotive sector, as well as the fact that the sources of some of the money that has entered this country are not clear. We have seen that the tension with the dollar increase after the decision to return some of this money to its source. This type of development model is dangerous. These factors trigger hopelessness and youth unemployment.

* * *

Dear Reader,

Istanbul, New York, San Francisco, Cape Town, Sydney, and Tokyo. Their most important common feature is that these cities are very expensive. Besides, the business life is much more difficult in these cities.

In the two additional sections at the end of the book, I will tell you about working in Istanbul and the depression that is created. In the other part, I will interpret the unemployment figures. Now, I want to start **"Real Professionalism"**, which is my main philosophy to explain to you. I don't want to lose more time.

Alper KUL

> "Expecting the world to treat you fairly because you are good is like expecting the bull not to charge because you are a vegetarian."
>
> Dennis Wholey*

---

* Dennis Wholey (born July 2, 1939, Cranston, Rhode Island) is an American television host and producer, and the author of a number of self-help books, one of which was a New York Times bestseller. He currently hosts This is America & The World with Dennis Wholey, an interview program shown throughout the U.S. on public television stations and the American Life TV Network.

2

FIRST TRUTH: TIME AND TIMING MANAGEMENT

– **You are mentioning Cave Symbolism in your seminars...**
– Yes, Plato in his cave allegory, which in the history of philosophy is quite famous, explains the difference between the "awake" person and the "sleeping" person.

> "Some people are sentenced from both to sit chained inside a dark cave facing away from the door. The people who are not able to turn their heads to the rear watch the shadows (made by means of the light that enters through the mouth of the cave and lights the opposite wall) of the other people and the things they carry when they pass by the entrance. One of them is freed, goes outside and sees the actual source. He then reenters and begins to explain what he has seen, but it is impossible to convince those inside that what they see on the walls are actually reflections and that reality occurs outside."

What does Plato want to communicate? "It is possible to see the truths, it's only possible when you get rid of the chains and get out of the cave to daylight." For, **"awakening"** is exiting the cave. Those who are able to awaken are seeing things as they truly are outside the cave and in the light of day.

For Plato, this great difference and the onerous situation is nothing more than the wisdom to distinguish the difference between how things appear and what is comprehended.

– **What does this wise discernment provide us?**

– It provides this difference: at the right time and at the right place, those countries like ours where life is difficult, we need to leave the cave and observe early on the way things are going and provide some possibilities for shortcuts, whether it's related to certain sectors, is economic or is concerning the near future.

What I want to say is that we need to be people who are somewhat **wise.** Otherwise, there's the possibility that we could take some big hits, of which I'm going to talk about next. You can enter the side or the dead-end streets. One has to be very careful. **It's very important to select the correct road and to continue on it persistently.**

– **What do you think lies at the core of being successful in work life?**
– When you look from the outside at work life, it appears quite complex. Yes, there are those aspects: difficult and complicated. From morning to night, the human factor is in play. Because of that, work becomes harder and precarious.

But I'm always saying this: if we develop ourselves toward being a real professional, and while still in school we orient ourselves to thinking that we will be a real professional in the future, then to not succeed is due to chance.

At this point, above all, I want to know this: **"As it is with all work, there are rules to being a professional and not an ordinary worker."**

First of all, we need a description. **Who is the professional person?**

A real professional:

- Is fond of his freedom.
- Is the worker who uses his mind best.
- Is never a slave.
- A majority of the rope is in his hand.
- It's not a big issue to look for and find work.
- A good professional, no matter what, doesn't work at just any job like an ordinary worker. He accepts work that will bring himself to his life's goals and grand ideal.

If we go further...

- Five years into his career, a real professional doesn't seek work for himself, it comes to him.
- In order to take the right steps toward professionalism and to be a real professional, there are 3 foundational truths. I will share these truths with you.
- Without being a professional, it is not possible to take steps toward leadership. First one becomes a professional and later a leader.
- A real professional is one who uses his mind and self-control more than a regular worker.

– **Without the "mind" it's impossible, you're saying...**
– That's exactly what I'm saying. In fact, in the seminars that I give on this topic, I frequently point out words related to "MIND". We must always use our minds. We must develop mechanisms in order to use it more. In one on one counseling sessions and workshops, I refer to and teach the "Mind Mapping" technique. Later if the topic comes up, I'd like to talk about a portion of this.

– **Isn't enough that we receive years of education?**
– You said it well. **Have you ever thought about what education is?** Education is a long period. In fact, in principle is based on a very basic thing: **the skill of using your mind.**

It's that simple, nothing else. If we are to summarize: **on the road to professionalism, after receiving so many years of education, the ability to use your MIND.**

What I want to say, we receive an education. Great. We also learned foreign languages. This is also good. However, there's something that's not right. We are keeping our empty dreams (not well-designed dreams), feelings, in the forefront of our minds, and we are acting contrary to the realities of our ecosystem.

What do you think the result could be?

– **Pain and broken dreams.**
– Exactly.

> "Wisdom is only found in truth."
> Johann Wolfgang von Goethe*

---

* Johann Wolfgang Goethe (28 August 1749 – 22 March 1832) was a German writer and statesman. His body of work includes epic and lyric poetry written in a variety of metres and styles; prose and verse dramas, memoirs; an autobiography, literary and aesthetic criticism; treatises on botany, anatomy, and colour; and four novels.

If we listen to Goethe's words, there are three basic truths for the person preparing for work life and to be a wise professional.

– **At this stage, if we listen to the words of the great German writer Goethe, with what truths do we need to fill our minds?**
– What does it mean to be wise? To be wise is not to stubbornly go down a wrong road and in the end, say, "He did great work but wasn't able to be successful." isn't it?

To be wise is to be strategic.

Later I'm going to talk about strategic intelligence. However, to be wise doesn't mean that you are always going to win. Success is something that comes with many factors coming into place.

Now I'm going to give the first truth for becoming a true professional:

The first truth of becoming a real professional at work and to be successful is **time & timing management**

In some seminars, I start with a time management survey. I receive the results right away and then at that moment the participants understand the qualities of "time management".

– **I don't believe that we are able to manage time. I believe that in today's conditions time is not under our control.**
– I believe exactly the opposite. Today I am a person who lives alone, and I have a lot of time to myself. But I've also had this happen to me a lot.... If I don't discipline myself and I come off the rails, then I see that I am able to come to the point where I'm not making time for my most basic needs. Here, the basic principle is **priorities**: to best determine your priorities and to not spend time on wrong and worthless things.

For a professional and even a professional student, a housewife, an apartment manager, a mechanic, a pilot and all workers and students the **most critical success factor: it is "time and timing management"**.

– **We know a little about time management but what kind of system is timing management?**
– Actually, there's a major difference between "time" management and "timing" management.

I will explain it briefly in this way. It is said that the concept of time is actually something we humans made up isn't. Is that so? Or is time actually something that is in the universe? Physicists, particularly Einstein, proved that it existed. There is a time in the universe. Whether we exist or not, it's there. Nevertheless, the period of our perception of **time** comes at the same period of our beginning to better understand ourselves and the universe. From my perspective, we understand time better after ages 7 and 8.

A period time, it is almost like a theater stage. We go onto the stage, we present our play, and we leave the stage. In this sense, the accompanying factor is **location**. Time exists only if there is a **location** ... No matter who it is, everyone leaves this theater stage. Even if "transhumans" succeed at extending our lives, time passes in an instant. Even if we live 150 years, it won't actually change too much.

So, then what should we do? We need to view this time as capital. This is what I want to say, the first 30 years of someone's life are very critical. Of course, the second 30 and the third 30 are also important, but the most important is the first 30 years.

– **Why?**
– It's very basic. What you do in those 30 years is what you are going to do. Primary school, middle school, high school, university or professional studies and other skills...sports, art, intellectual pursuits will be knitted together at these ages.

Those who take big steps after 35 or 40 are so few they can be counted on one hand. It's nearly impossible, especially in a career.

Because work life assumes that up until turning 30, you have long since prepared and have received all the education that you can.

However, as "Mr. Career", again I am saying that people need to be full of hope and shouldn't view age 35 as half way, but that as needed, believe that their careers and lives can be enriched by taking appropriate steps by receiving education and training.

This isn't impossible. The system I wanted to talk about is what the world and specifically the capitalist system expects from you. In this sense, my basic advice to young people is this: make the most of the ages 15 to 30. I'm not saying to not let them enjoy life. Let them eat, drink, play sports, but no matter what, at the forefront, our 5-wings windmill that we explained is being built during these ages. They did it! They did it! Otherwise, the second 30 years and the third 30 years might not be so enjoyable.

Or if I need to reverse it, if you sow throws the correct seeds to the ground during the first 30 years, and especially the first 20 years, and if you water this sprout well in your 20s, the 30s and between 30 and 60 will pass quite enjoyable. In this way, in a sense, you can buy and build the future.

You will manage the time or somebody else will manage you all! This world is this unequivocal and merciless.

In a sense, the time management does not direct just what we do in a day, but more than that how we make the most of the months and years. You always have things to do until evening, but now it's time to think like a developed society. People in developed societies think long term. They experience time in a broader way. However, in most of the developing societies, there is always a sense of urgency and haste reigns.

In developing societies, the people think short or middle range, and when we look at it, there's always a rush to get some place. Because the work that will be done will be, of course, partly short term. But in these types of societies, a very large portion of the work being done is short term.

There is no planning, no order and not any discipline. And time management is in a shabby state. In societies that think broadly about time, there is an order. There are fewer people who are in a rush. Of course, there is a tempo, but it is the difference between having a particular pace and being in a rush. Furthermore, in rushed systems, quality decreases. The developing societies most of the time are hasty and not paced.

Look, the quality arises only if your work designed comfortable and systematic way. I bet you that person who is hasty and always in a hurry will say that he/she will never be able to complete the work in 24 hours.

It's unbelievable, isn't it? But this type of person is everywhere. In fact, you even could be this way.

– Yes, I suppose that my time management isn't the greatest!
– I understand. **Timing management** is something different. Sportspeople know this quite well. In sports, no matter what branch of sport you are in, generally success has to do with **"timing"**. In other words, to pass the ball, at the right time in the right place to the right person, in general, has to do with timing.

In the past, I was a basketball player. I played on U19 teams. In basketball, timing is amazingly important. Most particularly if you are playing in the guard position, you must know the job well. You have to make good use of time both vertically (timing) and horizontally (time management). If you can't perceive and manage them, then you can't be a good basketball player. Be careful. A good coach will immediately remove you from the team.

Life is also like that. To know what you are going to do and when and take action based on that is **timing management**.

For example, in your work life, if you need to talk to your boss about a problem, even in this case there's timing. Every issue, every complaint, and every problem can't be addressed at that moment. Or, in the reverse, it needs to be addressed immediately, right at that moment. This time if you wait, it means you didn't practice good timing. So, what is needed in the work life?

– **You need to be an expert time and timing manager. However, timing management is hardly mentioned in writing. I've heard of books coming out on time management, but this is the first time I'm hearing about the importance of timing management.**
– It's normal for you to not have heard of it. Because in our societies, whether it's in our schools or in life, what is generally explained and shown to us is a limited concept of time. Like what I described earlier...to do everything very quickly...for example our exams. Exams are a real-time monster, aren't they? In 3 hours, your fate changes. University entrance exams or other exams like them are a timed rally. How you did in 3 hours! All the ingenuity is there. Actually, the best time management happens during exams.

But now I think that **"test taking"** is quite outdated. Now every servant of God understands that all of a person's skills and capabilities cannot be determined in a 3-hour exam (or a series of exams). This, actually, is an indication of falling behind.

No one gets upset at me. On several fronts, it's simple to understand if someone is talented in a certain area or not. But let's leave it there. Let the experts determine this with certain methods and clandestine or special test in time travels.

I'm asserting that every person definitely has one or more skills in an area. You can be very capable in at least one area. The issue is to have this brought out and have it be developed.

– **Technically, what are you recommending?**
– There are many principles. These need to be known at least in theory. These primarily come from the famous Italian scholar Vilfredo Frederico Damaso Pareto. The name of the famous Pareto's principle is that of his father. Have you heard of him?

– **I haven't.**
– I'd like to mention a bit about Signor Pareto. He actually studied physics and mathematics. Later he earned his doctorate from Torino Technical University. The best part is that he worked in the iron-steel industry. This is important. It's important that he was involved in work life.

In this way, he tested the application of theoretical knowledge. Later he began to develop economic theories. I found this interesting. His physics and mathematics knowledge certainly was very helpful in his analysis of Economics.

In economics, there is a school of thought called the "Lausanne School". This school of thought was named after "Leon Walras" along with the founder of the school. The methods of mathematical analysis were applied to the Statistics Theory. New insights were brought to expenditures, production, and other theories. Pareto asserts that trajectory, without relation to time and space, on the upper levels of the graph that shows the income distribution of each of the countries always stays the same, thus forming the Pareto chart or law. He was both a philosopher and a sociologist. At the same time, like I said, he was an economist and a basic scientist.

This gentleman has many calculations that benefit our task, but the most important is the Pareto Principle of time management.

Pareto Principle: On the topic of priorities, it's a very important work. As I determined earlier, time management is actually a management of priorities. It's nothing other than that.

Of course, there is the basic advice I had previously mentioned: **the mind. To use the mind...if we use our minds properly, then it will inform our priorities.** Now if we could return to the Pareto Principle...

According to, the Pareto Principle, of the total units in a group, the important units only make up a small section. Dr. J. M. Juran* applied this hypothesis that had come out to the area of quality control. In later times, Juran gave the name "Pareto Principle" this rule which can be used not only in quality control but also in other aspects of life.

The Pareto diagrams are used to determine the causes for problems and their degrees of importance. In quality control, it can be used to list according to the importance the reasons behind increasing faulty production and customer complaints. A characteristic of the diagram, in general, is that it verifies the Pareto Principle. In a sense, we could say that J. M. Juran is the father of

---

* Joseph Moses Juran, was born in the year 1904 in Romania. In 1912, he immigrated to the United States. He graduated from the Department of Electric Engineering at Minnesota University. Later he received his Doctorate of Law from Loyola University in Chicago. Along with William Edwards Deming, he played a very important role in the spread of Total Quality Management in the United States and Japan. In 1981, he was awarded the "Order of Sacred Treasure" by the Emperor of Japan, Hirohito. Juran, published very important works in the field of Total Quality Management. His work titled Juran's Quality Control Handbook is regarded as a classic and one of the most important works in the arena of Total Quality Management. In addition to these, he also published many books and articles. In addition, Juran defended the principle known as the "Pareto Principle". The Pareto Principle is known as the 80/20 rule. Juran defended the teaching that percent of problems are caused by 20 percent of causes. To summarize, a majority of the causes for problems result from a small percentage. (Source: Wikipedia)

quality control. Juran modeled this quite well while inspecting quality systems. Juran used the expressions **"the vital few"** and **"the trivial many"**. In this way, for example, 20 percent of a factory's products (either 20 percent of the product's components or 20 percent of the time spent producing those products) produce 80 percent of the total profit. In the same way, 20 percent of the workforce does 80 percent of the productive work. For example, 20 percent of the participants in a meeting monopolize the time of the 80 percent. Pareto explained this with his diagrams. Juran, however, integrated it into manufacturing productivity and quality systems.

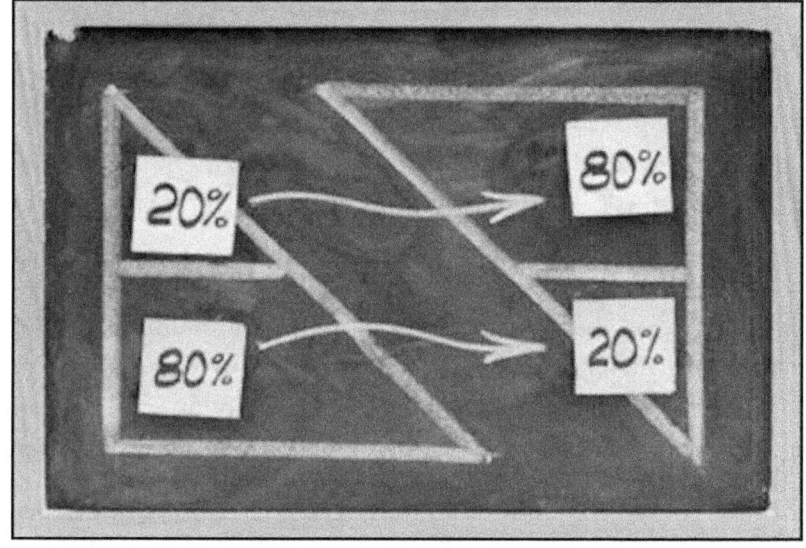

We call this also "80 to 20 rule". This is a clearer expression.

Signor Pareto's developed time principle indicates that inside a system, some elements that make up that system have a propensity to provide greater output than other elements. **From the time management aspect, the 80 percent of the success, it's coming from the 20 percent the time that dedicated for that work.** Here, the issue is to consider which of the 20 percent sections of time caused our productivity. In this way, we can say that it's possible to make specific evaluations of the unproductive 80 percent that is not creating results.

– **I didn't quite understand!**
– Now, I'm giving you a chart and a more basic explanation. As you can see here, it means that no matter what you are doing in life, of all the time your useable time, you are actually doing your most important work during 20 percent of it.

Or conversely, 80 percent of the time you are giving your time to unproductive work, and these give you 20 percent of the output.

For example, if sleep 8 hours, that leaves 16. In big cities, if 2 of these are spent on the road, that leaves 14. If you'll notice, in personal affairs and in our work lives, actual productivity includes 3-3.5 of this 14 hours.

Or in an 8-hours work day, the first 1 or 1.5 hours (or in total 1.5 hours) are the most productive hours. That is 20 percent of it. It means 20 percent of the total amount of time is functional. Workers that worked so many years do know this very well. A solid 2-hours work tempo in the morning hours actually makes the whole day. And that's the way it is. The service sector aside, this is especially true for sectors that include office professionals, marketers, salespeople, general management professionals, decision makers, and a significant section of the white-collar workers. Even in the service sector, the 20 percent productivity rate usually holds true.

– **So, people that many hours in vain?**
– That's not what I'm implying. I'm saying that only those hours are actually productive. This is especially true in our day since the computer entered our lives and made it easier (?).

Don't believe the many workers who say that I work 8 hours and can't (even) scratch my head. It means that there definitely is a problem with productivity. Or it means that companies, saying they have too many workers, have loaded these people with too much unnecessary work, resulting in a lack of productivity and an unsustainable tempo. William Whately said it like this: *"An hour lost in the morning will cause a whole day of disadvantage."* We must always keep this saying in mind.

– **So, in addition to this, are there other methods?**
– For example, there's "The Parkinson Principle". In a similar fashion, an inference from what is known as the "Parkinson's Law" states: **"How much time you have to complete a job, that's how much time it will take to finish."**

Let's say that I give myself 3 days to prepare an article for a presentation. I would have taken 3 days to write the article, but in reality, could have finished it in 3 hours.

– **Under pressure!**
– Exactly. Actually, when a person is pressured, his productivity increases. However, this is different than being hasty and rushed, as I mentioned previously. It has to do with using the "horizontal time" more productively. It's a rule to point out the amount of time capital that you give yourself. It's a matter related to bringing your flexibility under control.

The reason I mention the Parkinson rule is that, in a sense, it completes the "80/20 Pareto rule". And lastly, if you need to make some changes in your life in order to carry it to a higher level of quality and in order to realize your dreams of excellent time management, I recommend you apply basic strategies. These may look like rules that are given to students who are going to take a university exam, but actually, these, especially the capitalist systems of our day, are necessary time management rules. These rules are universal and have been tested.

Now:

- When working, don't be divided. We are saying don't give permission to being divided. This is basic. The most basic rule.
- Eliminate tasks. Don't do unimportant tasks. There will always be unimportant tasks.
- Provide a way to not have to return to the eliminated tasks. Otherwise, we can say, what did I understand from this task?
- Don't try to do every job. Delegate them to appropriate people. This is a life preserver for those you are very busy. Dele-

gation. But, of course, with the condition of finding the right people.
- The work you can do, do on time. Do it and finish it. But do it.
- Determine a production date for work that will be done later.

"Wise men learn more from fools than fools from the wise."

Marcus Porcius Cato*

---

* A Roman statesman, lawyer and orator (234-149 BC).

3

THE SECOND TRUTH: SPECIALIZATION

– We've explained in a comprehensive way that time management is a necessary thing. You mentioned three truths. Accordingly, could we move on to the second foundational truth?
– Of course, the second truth in order to be successful in your work life and to be a "real professional" is **specialization**.

– **Doesn't specialization necessitate a solid education?**
– Exactly, it is needed. For specialization, a lot of education might even be needed. The basic issue here is which area you specialized and in the course of this process which levels you passed. This is the important thing.

– **Is it possible to specialize in every field?**
– In each of the professions, it is possible to specialize in branches and achieve a certain depth working in different sectors.
  Work life is relentless...
  However, true experts can keep up in the work place. Sectoral and economic fluctuations don't affect a professional who has specialized in the right and strategic areas. For example, there are many subspecialties related to IT (Information Technologies) systems. Actually, every profession branch has its subcategories. In fact, like IT, fields like health, since, relatively speaking, they have newer branches, greater depth, and importance, sub specialties are more apparent and greater in number.

- **Just when I was going to ask you about the certificate legend, you began to mention it!**
- Ah, yes. In most of the societies, there are unbelievable legends on the topic of certificates! From the womb to the tomb everyone is running after a certificate. Of course, this is normal. If you remember what I said at the beginning, we talked about the world of "hope" for a person, and we said it didn't exist. The people cling to certificates as if they are life preservers. They think that they will be able to find work with certificates. Actually, they are right. If there were a standard in certificate programs and the task of education was taken seriously, then these certificates should be viewed as a key, but it's not that way.

    This business cannot be taken lightly. I'm going to tell you about a grueling certificate program. Have you ever heard of the CISSP?

- **What does it stand for?**
- **"Certified Information Systems Security Professional".** It is an independent certificate given by the ISC. According to the data from November 2016, this certificate, who 110.980 people in the world from 162 countries had received. The yearly average of 10,000 people is receiving it. I think this is a decent number.

    Likewise, on June 2004, the CISSP program ANSI ISO/IEC 17024:2003 was the first IT certificate to earn accreditation. It is a certificate recognized by United States Department of Defense in regard to the administrative and technical. This is important because it increases its universal quality in a sense. We know that it speaks to 8 foundational units of shared knowledge.

    From 2015, the CISSP curriculum is divided into eight domains:

    Security and Risk Management
    Asset Security
    Security Engineering
    Communications and Network Security
    Identity and Access Management
    Security Assessment and Testing

Security Operations

Software Development Security. Before 2015, it covered ten similar domains.

The right to receive the certificate is earned by taking an approximately 6-hours exam. It is required that at least a score of 700 is received on the exam. Two hundred and fifty questions are asked on the exam. In order to take the exam, at least **5 years** of experience working in information security is desired.

In this way, as I'm always asserting, one of the foundational truths of becoming a real professional, also shown by this extremely important certificate program, is the 5-years maturing period.

A 4-years undergraduate or master's degree from a related department is enough. Or other certificates obtained from other organizations is needed. With education and experience combined, it translates into a personal history of approximately 9-10 years. Naturally, their legal history must be clean since they will be looking after security systems.

Most importantly, they need to bring a reference from a professional in the sector who has already received a certificate from the CISSP. This is much more important since a reference is the most vital criteria for learning about the person. The best part is that the person who will give the reference is already CISSP certified.

Of course, to some friends, this certificate could come across as extreme, but it actually isn't. Today, those who've graduated or will from many different branches, not only in the computer but also information technology management, basic sciences and engineering sciences, these certificates are the target certificates. *"Certificates like CISSP are real certificates."* Their value is high. But in the end, they are a near guarantee of success and a lot of money. Of course, if you notice, behind every certificate there is a serious sense of **"goal consciousness"**. I will talk about this topic in the coming phases of our conversation.

* * *

"Wisdom is capital for a person."

A Turkish Proverb

* * *

– **Why are 5 years critical in work life and in general?**
– Do you know how many years you have to fly to learn to fly a plane properly? You must fly for thousands of hours. It's not something that happens in a matter of months. It means flying for years. In order to receive some certificates, they want from you 1500 hours of flying experience. The rules of the system in order to fly to be a pilot are among the most straightforward.

Becoming a doctor is also that way. You are going to study 6 years in medical school. That's not enough. Later you will devote 4-5 years to specialization. In a total of 10 years, you will become a "professional".

This might confuse people, but I'm not seeing a difference in the period it takes for a doctor to become experienced than a good engineer, or a good fireman, or a taxi driver who knows the streets well. In every branch...almost every branch 5 years is needed. Furthermore, it's important as to how those 5 years are spent. Is it spent in active vocational development or years spent in vain?

– **It's difficult, isn't it?**
– We're talking about becoming a real professional and building a career under normal conditions. Of course, it's difficult and troublesome. What good thing could possibly come easily?

– **It's my understanding that the programs that you mentioned earlier are very expensive. Where are people going to find this money?**
– That's a good question. This is a perfect investment. Do you want to have a profession? A real profession? One with validity? To accomplish this, before everything, you will emerge from the cave of many years ago. Your awareness will increase. You will feel the state of affairs in the world and in the country. If you are a graduate from high school or University, then you also need to

know where you are going (goal) after graduation and how you are going to get there. A person who has **"goal conscious"** will ultimately have a sound career.

The more our consciousness increases our goals and aims can change; their form is able to change. In this sense, goal consciousness is a dynamic process. I dreamed it and I did it! It's not simple as its.

Furthermore, when this goal mindfulness is present but the certificates are 400 or 800 USD, what's the use of them? This is why you will work many years, and you will put money away. As I said, you will make an investment. Or you will work to find a scholarship. In the end, the time you spend to find a scholarship is also an investment.

This question must always be asked in specialization: **Is my profession, first and foremost, a solid one across the country and one in which money can be made?** Or is there average professional formation? Or is there none?

For the next step, you need to ask this: **does my profession have international validity?**

– **That's a little bit fantastical, don't you think? If only we could find work in our country first!**
– That's not how it is. In our day, as I fully explained earlier, there is an amazing competition. Your today's profession might be less valuable tomorrow or could become completely worthless. Actually, we are in the age of continual learning and development. In this sense, the day may come when you will need to work in another country.

For example, civil engineering or technician jobs are this types of thing. Paying respects to our building contractors...a portion of them works outside the country. A portion of them knows Russian / Arabic / English. A big portion doesn't. But you may need to know it in your profession. You are going to research this. For example, it may be necessary to learn Arabic. I don't know. According to the profession or specialization, additional formation (education) may be needed.

In short, what I want to say is this: we need to perceive ourselves as being pilot or a specialized doctor! Look, I went to a vocational high school. I went to University, studied and even I did MBA. These were in the past, but now they have little value.

4

THE THIRD TRUTH: COMMUNICATION, RELATIONSHIPS SKILL MANAGEMENT, AND SOCIAL INTELLIGENCE

– I have some information on the topic of specialization, but I want to ask more questions on this topic in our future conversations. I want to move on to the third foundational truth. What is the 3rd standard for being successful and becoming a real professional?

– Yes, up until this time, I've shared with you the basics and essentials. These were "time management" and "specialization". These are characteristics a professional need.

When referring to a professional, for me, primarily, the image of a person who functions in a disciplined and orderly manner comes to mind. Who is the disciplined person? **The disciplined person is one who manages time well and keeps his/her word. When trusted with a job, finishes it no matter what, and if he can't finish it, gives warning at the right time.** In this sense, with the time management and specialization of a real professional worker lets us know that he/she is fundamentally very strong.

To be fundamentally strong doesn't necessarily mean that you will be successful in your work life. These qualities can give you access to any type of job. It can bring you to the point of being a good worker that is sought after. However, this doesn't make you a real professional in every sense. The 3rd and complementary truth toward becoming a real professional is **relationship management and social intelligence**.

– **Is it that important to always be able to get along with people? Isn't your work itself sometimes more important?**
– Relationship management does not always involve your relationships with people being good. Sometimes is the opposite.

I might surprise you. The thing called "social intelligence" is a very incisive and difficult thing. Here, sometimes personal politics enter in. Sometimes you need to say "no" to some things. At that moment, skills in relationship management kick in. You could have a fall out with the person who you say "no" to or that person might lose faith in you. You must manage this very well.

A real professional is almost like an actor. You can see this in verbal disputes. Or even if it's quite rare, one could come across as harsh toward a customer. But there definitely must be a reason behind this. It must be based on professional reasons and must be removed from emotional reasons.

If we go deeper into this subject what can we say? For one, whether it's in regard to new graduates or all experienced professionals, "communication skill" is the most foundational ability that they will use it the rest of their lives.

I must say this. In fact, even for an apprentice, it's unusually important. Because if an apprentice makes himself loved than he can stay in that system. In most cases, even though apprentices are short-term, they are brought in to fill openings in human resources. But all of a sudden, you look, and the apprentice starts working after graduation. Of course, at this time we assume the apprentice wanted to work there. Since in most cases there is a very little difference among apprentices, those who have the best communication skills are preferred, if there is no nepotism and favoritism at the company. This is how it should be.

– **When referring to "communication" what do we understand?**
– When referring to "communication", people assume we are talking about something that is one-sided. That is, merely those

people who get along with people well, don't have any psychological problems, are sympathetic, are always smiling able to understand you. No, like I said before, sometimes a sympathetic stubbornness can become a sign of communication acumen.

I've applied this a lot in my own work life. Sometimes I did not come across as sympathetic but rather disagreeable. To them, I needed to show a stubborn and driving stance. It's not always the right thing to be results-oriented. But, in the end, you are expected to deliver in business. But you ultimately are going to achieve this with your communication intelligence.

Furthermore, communication is not just verbal. In our day, when we refer to communication, we are talking about a very complex thing. Now, one of the best communication methods is to use social media and to use it well.

I imagine you are going to ask me soon to be about a "career in social media". Social media has a perfect spiral effect. It has begun to enter every part of our lives. Especially those in the 14 to 45 age group, if they don't have a Facebook, LinkedIn or Twitter account, then they are treated like a "virtual ignorant". This might seem like a harsh description, but unfortunately, the world trends are heading this direction.

– **So, Facebook or Twitter?**
– When referring to social media, let's be real, not too many sites come to mind. Those that do are primarily Facebook and Twitter. These dominate the system. According to the descriptions of the day, it is critical, especially for those between the ages of 18 and 45 to be present in these two systems.

If you are asserting that you are a true professional, and if you are young, your other young friends will follow you and will want to draw parallels between you and themselves. If you have Facebook and Twitter accounts, it will be easy for them to find similarities with you. If you don't, then they could accuse you of being asocial!

This may seem like a harsh remark, but I always speak from the perspective of a realist. Today, young people do not put down their cell phones, and especially smartphones. It means this: **Hey! I'm in this "space". If you are also "in this space", then I can communicate with you. Otherwise, no offense, but I'm not able to communicate with you.**

This is valid for "professionals". But I'm always saying this. Professionals must be very careful with their personal Facebook pages. I'm asserting that today personal Facebook pages can be accessed and some valuable information can be obtained.

In this case, to give an exact answer to your question: I say **"Facebook"**. Because in some aspects, the Facebook's method is easier and is a channel with a larger impact. Moreover, Twitter is an area that needs to be online every second, every minute, and if you have serious followers, you are affected. In Twitter, to get reasonable and effective followers you need a lot of **time**. If you sacrifice your time, of course, you can obtain some reasonable and serious followers. But except for some of the youth, professionals, especially the real professionals that we talked about, don't have this much time. When things are this way, the Twitter is not too much effective.

The other issue is related to that person's public personality. If you already have a place of influence, for example, if you are a famous pop star or football player, it means that you automatically have some group followers.

Actually, in the past, these people had public spokespeople and personal managers, and these people said what should be shared and what shouldn't be. They maintained relationships with the press. Now it's not that way. Actually, this case of communication management involves some drawbacks. Unexpected comments (with limited 140 characters) that you didn't especially plan, they can create real problems. In that sense, I'm saying that please be careful with Twitter postings. Communication management can turn into a communication disaster.

– **So, you're not recommending using Twitter?**
– No, that's not what I'm saying. However, I said it's appealing for someone who has a problem, one who has something they're

wanting to say, and for someone who has influence in the public arena. **Twitter almost functions as an attack machine and as a societal discharge station. But whether it's for community events or also other societal emergency communications, it's definitely desirable.**

However, I'm not sure how healthy it is to try to squeeze everything, every thought into 140 characters. Besides, for productive people, Facebook provides a much more attractive applications system and possibilities.

Some companies evaluate the writings, publications, and stances on the Facebook, Twitter and LinkedIn accounts of potential and even current employees. We may find this democratic or not. As time goes on, have no doubt they are going to look even more. If you were the boss and were looking for an employee for an important position, would you not have looked?

– **I suppose I would have.**
– Of course, in social media, there are methods for "camouflaging". However, no matter what, a person who wants to reach you ultimately will. There is a question in classic hiring and on personnel forms. Actually, that question is not well understood. They ask if you are a member of associations, clubs or social organizations.

From now on this question will change. Now, these questions will be asked: *"Which social media platforms are you a member of and in them what groups are you part of?"*

For example, today if I look for an employee from LinkedIn, I will easily understand this since I can see the large section in the profiles that show the groups a person is a member of. I can enter those groups and look at the what that person published, and I can make a detailed evaluation of that person. Today this is an especially critical responsibility that needs to be done by the intelligent human resources department.

– **I understand, so if we return to the topic, if we would want to rank the career websites, which is the most important?**

– Among these, **linkedin.com*** is different than the others. Actually, the basic question should be: are we talking about a white-collar worker or a worker with a different color of the collar? Are we just speaking of one of my blue-collar friends? The answer to these questions is important.

Today, since LinkedIn is mostly used in English and the philosophy regarding its establishment is more toward white-collar professionals, this platform speaks to workers at a certain level. Rather than a job search platform, it functions as a database. Today, in the world as of the second half of 2016, there are 467 million LinkedIn users. This means there are just about that many white-collar members.

The databases of most important head hunters in the world don't even have these many resumes, and due to their methods,

---

* LinkedIn is a business and employment-oriented social networking service that operates via websites and mobile apps. Founded on December 28, 2002, and launched on May 5, 2003, it is mainly used for professional networking, including employers posting jobs and job seekers posting their CVs. As of 2015, most of the company's revenue came from selling access to information about its members to recruiters and sales professionals. As of September 2016, LinkedIn had more than 467 million accounts, out of which more than 106 million are active. LinkedIn allows members (both workers and employers) to create profiles and "connections" to each other in an online social network which may represent real-world professional relationships. Members can invite anyone (whether an existing member or not) to become a connection. The "gated-access approach" (where contact with any professional requires either an existing relationship or an introduction through a contact of theirs) is intended to build trust among the service's members. LinkedIn participated in the EU's International Safe Harbor Privacy Principles.

The site has an Alexa Internet ranking as the 20th most popular website (October 2016). According to the New York Times, US high school students are now creating LinkedIn profiles to include with their college applications. Based in the United States, the site is, as of 2013, available in 24 languages, including Arabic, Chinese, English, French, German, Italian, Portuguese, Spanish, Dutch, Swedish, Danish, Romanian, Russian, Turkish, Japanese, Czech, Polish, Korean, Indonesian, Malay, and Tagalog. LinkedIn filed for an initial public offering in January 2011 and traded its first shares on May 19, 2011, under the NYSE symbol "LNKD".

On June 13, 2016, Microsoft announced plans to acquire LinkedIn for $26.2 billion. The acquisition was completed on December 8, 2016. The transaction resulted in the payment of approximately $26.4 billion in cash merger consideration. (Source: Wikipedia)

most of the time their databases are out of date. Actually, LinkedIn is not that way. There is an incredible dynamism, and every changing position, every new additional work being done, every activity, and every received training is written there. Have you ever thought about why it is this active?

– **Why?**
– Because as people look around on LinkedIn, they see that it is a serious platform and that people are serious. These are also people who have quite good English. In one sense, it's a *universal place*. Here, they say that the better and up-to-date we stay, we'll receive that much more return.

One of the most important parts of LinkedIn is the section called **"endorsement"** or **"recommendations"** containing short letters of recommendation. You are able to receive recommendation letters (or "reference") regarding any of your jobs or endeavors. This way, LinkedIn prevents classic methods like receiving reference numbers and calling the people.

Today, it may not be easy to for you to talk on the telephone a contact from a firm and give a reference for a worker that you worked with years before. You may have forgotten many details. I advise professional friends who are looking for work to use this recommendation letter (writing) section to the fullest. Headhunters read this one by one. Furthermore, like I said, LinkedIn might be able to be opened in different methods in the future. It can save in the background your success record, your brief success stories, in fact, your video where you describe yourself. Now, presentation by video has become started. Many people, including me, have begun to upload videos.

Even more, in the future as fiber optic systems become more widespread, as the internet speeds up, and its quality increases, they are going to want to do a live video interview with you. In this way, distances are made shorter. LinkedIn can develop a calling program for this function. This is a work search, database, and networking platform.

Furthermore, a section of one of the most important application is called "Skills & Expertise". People voluntarily indicate your characteristics as you've portrayed yourself. In this way, in a very easy way, they are tagging you. In this manner, your skills are endorsed by many more people. From my perspective, this is a simple and attractive innovation.

– **So, what if these recommendations and labels are fake and organized?**
– No, very few of these could be that way. This is for a few reasons. First, the Western mind doesn't think that way. But for some developing societies can.

Actually, this isn't a bad thing. No upper-level person will write or approve for another upper-level person a recommendation letter that he doesn't believe. That kind of thing isn't possible. Even if it is contrived, I don't find this to be wrong. In this arena, that kind of thing is possible. Let's leave it alone. Let people write what they think about each other. The problem could be here: these people only accept positive things and the negative things don't enter into play. Forgive me, but here, a kind an extension of the business world.

In the business life, which company says, "I'm bad. Oh no, I'm going down. This is a poorly managed and unprofitable company?" Everyone says, "Don't let it out of this room." For the love of God, then what is the fault of the workers and professionals?

Actually, the human resources people' real work is to sort through all of the these. They must separate out the ones that are from **outer space** from the ones that are good, and later who are truly good, who are over there for just only **"show!"**

Someone must do this. So, leave it aside. Let LinkedIn also determine the selection criteria and begin to recruitment selection tests! How correct that would be!

– **What else do you recommend on LinkedIn?**
– LinkedIn is actually, a vast expanse. I think any investment to be made in it is the right thing. There are different types of memberships. For example, there are memberships types that you can be a part of for very little money, such as "premium memberships". Here, the important thing is not your looking for a job, it's to take

advantage of the system. When you become a premium member, you can see who is searching for you and enter your profile. You can receive from the LinkedIn help desk much more professional and quick support. Although, again, you can't send a message to everyone and who you want, but this isn't that important (you can send to limited members InMail – direct message). Actually, in time the numbers of your connections increase and as your connections increase, geometrically you have more connections. In this way, you can connect with others via the system of recommendations.

Actually, outside of this, the features that I recommend are LinkedIn's professional and hobby groups. I recommend that you join these. This makes it easier for you to make connections with professionals who are at the forefront of their field. Because this feature on LinkedIn adds to your prospects that your professional connections will increase as you gain a place in the same group. This feature in LinkedIn provides the possibility of adding to your personal connections due to being in the same group. Or at least you can find more easily appropriate and more useful connections from hobby or professional network subgroups of LinkedIn.

– **Doesn't communication intelligence emerge from all of what you have explained?**
– Yes, exactly. You might be a great person, but you need to follow well your goals and subject matter on the internet and the platforms created by the internet. Even the internet you need to use well.

You need to understand their functions. Otherwise, you have difficulty when looking for quality work, and you leave the task to chance. Or it needs to be said this way: in order to increase your chances, you need to be on the internet.

– **I'm not sure if this is valid for LinkedIn, but the complaints that I receive most frequently today are from people who don't receive a response from job search sites. There is a serious frustration about these websites. What do you say about this topic?**

– I agree with these views to a large degree. This also happened to me in the past, and to a large degree for reasons stemming from the company, responses are not returned, even out of courtesy.

Now it is said that the internet has made our lives easier. However, the internet is substantive only as long as you are able to meet your needs. You place an ad. For example, you are going to hire an environmental engineer. This is the case. In most of the countries, there are many environmental engineers who cannot find a job and naturally want to do their own work. Even if these are only a small portion, if they apply, there is a risk that thousands of CVs will be waiting in the company application pool. What does a company do in this situation? Among the hundreds of people applying, they enter 2 criteria. They apply a filter, in order to find those who have graduated from METU* Environmental Engineering, those who have been working for the last 5 years and have gained experience.

So, let's say that we have 7 people left. Only these people are called. This might not be METU graduation, but the company could have had other criteria. The important thing is that companies must simplify and must manage their time well. Outside of that, some of them are sending an automated message. It's debated as to how classy and ethical that is, but we need to be thankful to those who do this. Since a large segment of companies doesn't even send an automated message.

– **So, I suppose we summarized the topic of a career on the internet or social media. Is there anything missing?**
– I'd like to summarize in this way. Social relations and internet usage support each other.

---

*   Middle East Technical University (commonly referred to as METU; in Turkish, Orta Doğu Teknik Üniversitesi ODTÜ) is a public technical university located in Ankara, Turkey. The university puts special emphasis on research and education in engineering and natural sciences, offering about 40 undergraduate programs within 5 faculties, and 97 masters and 62 doctorate programs within 5 graduate schools. The main campus of METU spans an area of 11,100 acres (4,500 ha), comprising, in addition to academic and auxiliary facilities, a forest area of 7,500 acres (3,000 ha), and the natural lake Eymir. METU has more than 120,000 alumni worldwide. The official language of instruction at METU is English. (Source: Wikipedia)

I am keeping an eye on developments in social media while we are talking, but in the end, I am continuing to talk with you. This is something that can be done. In fact, I see people with their phones open while exercising in the gym or even on the tennis court. I even see people talking while running if needed. To me, that is very crazy.

If you are doing a job that requires a lot of effort and concentration, you are going to do work on that job. Here, the only thing you need to do it is a break and relax. That's it.

Furthermore, I want to say this. Relationship management is multi-dimensional. If needed it might even require sending a postcard. It can't be said, "why is this necessary?" Some people like the classic letter and postcard. You must know well concerning what, to where, to whom it will be sent or what time it is necessary to cut off your relationship. Relationship management means to put it aside while not causing a problem and, if needed, to break off a relationship.

"The man who makes no mistakes does not usually make anything."

Edward John Phelps*

---

* Edward John Phelps (July 11, 1822 – March 9, 1900) was an American lawyer and diplomat from Vermont.

This isn't written in a classic self-development book because in classic instruction paints the picture of a type of person who gets along well with everyone and is agreeable. I don't accept this, and I'm saying what everyone knows but isn't exactly able to put into words. Sometimes you need to be bad, and you need to end the relationship. Or at least you need to freeze it. This is inescapable in professional and personal life. Otherwise, you wear down and can't make anyone happy. Here, the important thing is to be a good person, to not bring harm anyone or nature and to do your work in the best way possible.

Look, there is one person, not only in Turkey but among all the professionals in the whole world, who is extremely successful in the area of management and relationships with people. That person is the president of the Coca-Cola Company, the esteemed Mr. Muhtar Kent.*

Years ago, it was the year 2007 I suppose, Muhtar Kent participated as a speaker at "Retail Days" in Istanbul. There, he mentioned 3 fundamental lessons to which I had subscribed and had strengthened my theory.

Muhtar Kent is **real professional**. Of course, I will give other examples. Of course, when you give examples, you will look at the coherence and uniformity with the truths that I laid out earlier and their career journeys. Furthermore, we are not researching the most successful and the most social people. We are attempting to ascertain what a real professional is.

---

* In December 2016, Coca Cola announced that Kent would step down as CEO in May 2017, making way for COO James Quincey to take the top spot. Kent would continue as Chairman of the Board of Directors.

In this sense, "Turkish-American Muhtar Kent" is the most suitable person.

He reached this level of professional in 40 years, but I am in shock that there has not been serious research for an article or book written about him. Whereas, I think that one or more books should have come out with a perspective on Mr. Kent's extraordinary successes. Other books then maybe should criticize and bring in other perspectives.

If I had for years been working in a company that was Coca-Cola's rival, I would have been following Muhtar Kent from the beginning of the 1990s and would have been curious as to where he was going. I actually want to explain Muhtar Kent's life's journey in a book. If I could find an opportunity, I would like to have an in-depth interview with him. I will ask him about the 3 truths, and actually of course, outside of these, there are hundreds of questions that will be asked.

– **I am looking at the internet now, and there really isn't much worthwhile information!**
– It's interesting, isn't it? It's unbelievable. There are many American sources. For the interested, I want to give you a couple of

links and some quotes from Mr. Kent. Further, the best address will be Coca-Cola's official website:

http://en.wikipedia.org/wiki/Muhtar_Kent

Chairman of the Board:

http://www.coca-colacompany.com/our-company/board-of-directors-muhtar-kent

Sustainability strategy regarding on women:

http://www.coca-colacompany.com/stories/coca-cola-unites-with-top-consumer-companies-to-collectively-sou

> "Empowering women entrepreneurs and women-owned firms are smart business and smart economics."
>
> "Whenever you do the right thing and give business women a real opportunity to compete, this creates a positive ripple effect that allows her to strengthen her company, her family, and her community. And stronger families and communities help fuel more growth and opportunity."

Kent formed a Women's Leadership Council at Coke to promote the recruitment, retention, development, and advancement of female leaders. He also made it a priority to boost the number of women on the company's board of directors. As a result, 40 percent of senior posts at the company are now held by women, and the number of female directors has doubled, from two to four.

Recognizing the need to empower women outside the four walls of The Coca-Cola Company, Kent also spearheaded the 2010 launch of 5by20, an ambitious initiative to support the economic empowerment of 5 million women entrepreneurs globally by 2020.

> "Economically empowered women help make communities better around the world. And when communities get stronger around the world, global businesses become stronger."

Muhtar Kent: Why I Am a Feminist:

http://www.coca-colacompany.com/stories/why-i-am-a-feminist

Coke CEO Muhtar Kent advocates for gender equality at Women's Forum in France:

http://www.coca-colacompany.com/stories/coke-ceo-muhtar-kent-advocates-gender-equality-at-women-s-forum-in-france

Coca-Cola CEO Muhtar Kent receives 2017 Water Leader Award: http://www.coca-colacompany.com/stories/coca-cola-ceo-muhtar-kent-receives-2017-water-leader-award

Muhtar Kent's New Coke by Patricia Sellers – Fortune: http://www.coca-colacompany.com/stories/muhtar-kents-new-coke

Our Water Wakeup Call...What Will Be Yours?: http://www.coca-colacompany.com/stories/our-water-wakeup-call-what-will-be-yours

> "I predict that if you aren't responsibly managing water in your business, you won't be in business 20 years from now."
>
> "Water is one of the major issues that threaten the world we share and transcends the views we don't. Let this be your wakeup call instead of waiting for a drier one."

Building a Resilient Business in the Eye of an Economic Storm: http://www.coca-colacompany.com/stories/building-a-resilient-business-in-the-eye-of-an-economic-storm

Chinese Consumers Do a Double-Take as Warren Buffett Graces Cherry Coke Cans: http://www.coca-colacompany.com/stories/chinese-consumers-do-double-take-as-warren-buffett-graces-cherry-coke-can

(31 March 2017) Coca-Cola Chairman and CEO Muhtar Kent said he is pleased that the China business chose to launch Buffett's favorite drink in such a unique way.

> "I can't think of a better way to launch Cherry Coke than with its best-known fan on the package," Kent said. "It is an honor for us to be able to feature Warren on his favorite drink as it rolls out in one of the world's most exciting and dynamic consumer markets."

Yahoo Finance reported on how this all came about: *"Four or five months ago, Coca-Cola Chairman and CEO Muhtar Kent said they were going to introduce Cherry Coke into China and asked me about putting my picture on the cans and bottles,"* Buffett told Yahoo Finance. *"I said it would be fine to do it for the first six months after launching the product. If there are no problems associated with this and he asks me to continue, I will likely say OK. Incidentally, there is compensation involved.* For the drawing, Buffett said, *"I did no down for a portrait. I think Muhtar knew better than to ask for this; I've never been keen on that sort of activity."*

Except those mentioned above, for a general introduction, I want to submit to you his resume appearing on "cix1.info". This resume is short, plain and adjusted a little bit by me. Outside of this, as I said earlier, except for a few interviews, resources are limited.

"Muhtar Kent was born in New York City in the United States of America in 1952.

His father, Necdet Kent, was a famous ambassador known as "The Turkish Schindler."

In 1978 Muhtar Kent graduated from the economic department of Hull University in England where he had gone for education. In the same country, after completing a Master's in Business Administration at Case Business School, he returned to Turkey to fulfill his army duty.

After the army, he went to America and took up residence near his uncle. He found a job with Coca-Cola from a newspaper ad. Going from city to city, he sold coke from a Coca-Cola truck. He learned distribution, marketing, and the logistics system.

In 1985, he became the general manager of Coca-Cola Turkey and Central Asia. He moved the company's headquarters in Turkey from Izmir to Istanbul. Three years later he rose to become a vice president for Coca-Cola International, assuming responsibility for 23 countries from the Alps to the Himalayas.

He began to live in Vienna. This assignment lasted until 1995.

Promoted further, in 1995 Kent became the managing director of Coca-Cola Amatil- Europe. In 2 years, he increased turnover by 50 percent in 12 countries.

After completing 20 years with them, he left Coca-Cola in 1999. He didn't prefer to retire.

He went over to the Anadolu Industry Holding in Turkey. The highest-level manager of Efes Beverage Group had left the managing group, and he took on this position.

He broadened the company from the Adriatic to China.

After about 6 years of a break, he returned to the Coca-Cola Company in April of 2005. He became the president of North Asia, Eurasia, and the Middle East. Doing this, he assumed 1 of 6 equally important jobs just under the CEO. He was connected to giant countries like China, Russia, and Japan.

In 2006, Kent's rise continued. This time he was brought to the head of all of Coca-Cola's operations outside of North America.

Kent's success carried him to the summit in December 2007. **On July 1, 2008, Coca-Cola brought him to the top position of CEO.** This is the first time a Turk rose to the top of one of the most valuable firms.

The 8-armed octopus

Muhtar Kent married Defne Kent, a daughter of the internationally-famous Turkish lawyer, Professor Ilhan Lütem.

Defne Kent one described her husband as an 8-armed octopus during an interview. She said, "He does all the repairs at home. He's crazy about shopping. He loves flowers a lot. He walks our dog, Hamur, and his olive oil factory in Ayvalık is very important to him." The Kent couple has 2 children.

Sea Admirer:

Coworkers describe Kent as a "perfect manager". Known as quick thinking, a fast decision-maker and as focusing more on the results than the details, it is said that "he makes a goal and moves quickly to reach it."

Kent spends most of his time outside of work at the sea. Being from Ayvalık, Kent goes out on a boat, goes sailing and tries to be alone in nature when he finds opportunity.

Turkish Schindler:

His father Necdet Kent, The Turkish Schindler who passed away in 2002, was a Turkish diplomat appointed to France during the World War II.

Father Kent, while serving in Marseilles, saw the Germans forcefully gathering and loading the Jews into trains in order to take them to the extermination camps. He could not stand this inhumane treatment and he himself got on a train and convinced the German officer that those near him were Turkish citizens and thereby saved hundreds of Jews. Therefore, Necdet Kent was given the nickname "The Turkish Schindler."

In 2001 Necdet Kent was given a superior service medal by the Republic of Turkey Ministry of Foreign Affairs."

– **An unbelievable life story...**
– Yes, but like I said earlier, it's not well known. Yet, in the novel written by Ayşe Kulin titled "Breathless", which explains the Jews' suffering and the Nazi oppression during World War II, the character named "The Turkish Republic Marseille Consul General Nazım Kender" represents Necdet Kent. Those curious can read the novel.

Now I want to talk about from my perspective Muhtar Kent's best and clearest speech in Turkey which took place at the November 2007 "Retail Days". In this talk, Muhtar Kent gives very clear and radical information about the topic most important to me and on which I deliberate on: **relationship management.**

I have serious doubts and concerns regarding globalization. I'd like to explain these concerns at a later time. However, Muhtar Kent touches on it in this way:

Muhtar Kent in his amazing speech titled **"Managing a Company on Which the Sun Never Sets"** explains in a very clear way the experiences he has had up until that point and the lessons he learned.

We can summarize these 3 basic lessons with titles:

Lesson 1: **There isn't a Global Template**

> "There's a paradox in globalization: the equal rise of local cultures and values along with globalization."

This is what I mean. Globalization in this sense is both theory and philosophy with false and missing identification. Muhtar Kent summarized this well.

And, said these words:

> "The most important information from the market is information obtained "first hand". This information's place isn't held in reports or research. Our most important task is to browse every market where we show activity and to talk and establish relationships."

You see? At that time while explaining how important relationship management is in my seminars, the words of Muhtar Kent caught my attention and as is began to use them in my seminars. Muhtar Kent summarized with one sentence what I had racked my brains over for years.

The way to success is if and only if it is possible to establish and design good relationships. Otherwise, no matter how good you are, in the end, you are banging your head against a wall.

Lesson 2: **To Work with the Right Person**

> "An upstanding person is someone who has a concept of the world, has the courage to go outside of his comfort zone and frequently does, is able to operate among cultures and is able to learn while taking risks."

I say underline the words above. If you want to be successful in the 21st century, then you will give ear to these words. **"Comfort and Comfortableness"** that is the ability to be at ease and relaxation, was the title of I explained at the 4th Mediterranean Management Summit. The things Muhtar Kent explained weave in with mine.

There is another paradox in globalization: As people become richer, they are seeking an easier and more comfortable life. They want this in every area. Consider shopping and places where parking is easily found. The bed that you sleep and the chair in the plane you board.

Only, the paradox I'd like to point out is this: people while on one hand wanting an easier life, a large number of people are faced with a less comfortable work life. And as Muhtar Kent pointed out, a significant portion of large companies want you to leave your **comfort zones.**

There is a big contradiction here, but both are true. Large and assertive firms demand more sacrifice from you. Sacrifices are able to be made. You are able to work anywhere in the world and you are able to adapt to difficult situations, however, what's important is this: are you able to be rewarded?

This is the problem: a capitalist system doesn't behave in a democratic way toward everyone because its construction isn't conducive toward that. If everyone receives a high premium, then the system breaks down. However, in the past, there were other problems. This issue of promotion always creates a problem. Naturally, it will also happen a thousand years later. Since in hierarchical systems, this is a natural problem.

– **In this case, what should be done?**
– Actually, there are many things that can be done. For example, you can make your own pyramid or you can move on to another pyramid (to a company, set up, system, organization or civil society). True, a system has its own bottlenecks, but it also has its own valves for opening and broadening. We can analyze these points in depth in another conversation.

– **Concerning the 2nd lesson, there are a lot of things to talk about...**
– Exactly. What does Muhtar Kent say? To have a **"World Perspective.."**. What do you think that means?

– **One who has a philosophy, a structure of thought...**
– Absolutely. It means one who has climbed on a branch. One who puts forth the effort to understand the world and his environment and actually is the intellectual that I had described earlier.

He's saying if the worker does not have a world perspective then we won't be able to receive an output from him.

– **Someone who is able to function among cultures...**
– Yes, this is another important truth. Today, global companies can have no dealings with workers who are locally-minded and look at events from a local perspective. This is normal. **Global companies work with "global people".**

Today, a Pakistani, a Turk, a Senegalese and an Arab can work anywhere and can adapt quickly to the society to which he has gone. Or it is expected to be this way. You can't be like the local people. The important thing is not to imitate and try to live like them. The priority is to respect and to try to understand that culture where you have gone to live and work. This is what Muhtar Kent is trying to say. To be people and workers who are respectful of other cultures and are able to integrate into them but to actually never lose their identity...

– **He also says that the person who learns while taking risks is a true person. Are large companies truly taking risks or are the providing opportunities for their workers to take risks? Can this type of thing be said?**
– Very good question. Yes, large companies don't like people who take personal and irresponsible risks. In fact, Muhtar Kent says this expressly. Actually, large companies take large risks. This is why there isn't a real place for personal risks. However, in every risk-taking, there is a creativity and a compulsion. Or at least this is how we expect it to be. Muhtar Kent has other interviews on this topic. It will mention them to you later.

Muhtar Kent asserts that large companies should be managed like small companies. In his opinion, the demand to feel the need for workers who can take **"responsible and intelligent"** risk is because of this.

This is a good thing and also keeps one active in the culture. Actually, no matter what, large companies are systematic companies. In this sense, there is a need for employees who are brave and willing enough to take a risk (but not illogical irresponsibility). Cowardice is a false feeling.

– Do you think they are able to be found?
– I think they aren't able to find them. Actually, this is where the problem is.

The system and powers that are managing the systems are not so willing to find and develop the upcoming human capital who are able to take risks, are open to different experiences, the worker profile that Muhtar Kent desires.

– Why?
– I think this question needs to be asked, not of me but of system managers.

At this time in companies, my observation is that there are serious problems with creativity and management. These are actually connected with each other. This will be the result if you don't bring into company's people who have the ability to think differently and have the personality to question and if you bring in the **nominal manager**, the manager profile that I described. That is, the situation **"manager in title, not in person"**.

Today, not only in developing societies but in the world, there is an employer-manager conflict and employers always want managers who only listen to what they say or are loyalty to the generally accepted systems. Because of this, the viewpoints and stance of Muhtar Kent, who is at the top of one of the largest companies in the world, are important.

– I understand. So, what is the 3rd lesson?
– Lesson 3: **The Ability to Establish Long-Term Relationships**

> *"It is actually possible to know that a long-term associate, a work partner, will be by your side in a moment of crisis. Companies that are considered to be "global" are able to be become localized due to long-term relationships,"* Muhtar Kent says.

In addition to this, I also maintain in my seminars that just as every professional person is forced to establish long-term relationships, the companies that manage them also must be able to build long-term relationships with their environments.

What did I say? The 3 truths of a real professional come to hand. **Time management, specialization and "relationship management and social intelligence"** ...

Muhtar Kent thinks of "global companies" as relationship machines. So, who will manage these companies? From my perspective, people who have these 3 characteristics must manage. That is, real professionals and those who have leadership qualities...

I call these people "real managers". I am always using this sentence: "First one become a professional, later a leader."

– **You said that Muhtar Kent maintains that large companies should be managed like small companies...**
– For years, I have been following the writings and analyses of leading reporter for *Capital* magazine, Mr. Rauf Ateş. In the November 3, 2009, issue of Posta magazine, one of his articles was published. I am submitting this piece writing for your attention:

> *"The Need to Manage Like a Small Operation...*
>
> *The guest of the Monday morning breakfast, brought about by our Capital and Economist magazines' CEO Club, was Muhtar Kent. Turkey's leading CEO (upper management) and businessmen came together to listen to the important manager of the 80 billion-dollar Coca-Cola company. Before the breakfast, while discussing the program, I asked for his views on a certain topic.*
>
> *After Muhtar Kent's speech, at another activity, I had a presentation related to Mid and Small size enterprises managers. Since I knew the difficulties of motivating the owners of small operations, as well the owners of large operations, I wanted to relate Muhtar Kent's message to them.*
>
> *My question has been this:* **"Is there differences between the management of a small operation and that of a large operation? What is a common aspect of each?"**
>
> *Both must be managed as if they were small!*
>
> *Muhtar Kent's response was like this:*
>
> *"Every day I recommend my associates at Coca Cola that they manage the large company as if it were a small operation.*

Because small operations are more agile, flexible and quick. Their dynamism and capacity to achieve unity should be imitated. That is why, at every opportunity, I am going out and observing the retailers and grocers. Every month I spend 2 to 3 of my hours with the sellers. In order to understand change, I am trying to observe the way they work. In the end, whether it's small or large... both are operations. The characteristics of the ones that are small, not the large ones, that need to be focused on."

The 2 Essential Responsibilities of Leaders:

I have shared this vision of Muhtar Kent with small business owners. There was a lot of interest. Some, "Is it possible to have any similarity between small and large?" they objected. Actually, in general, a positive atmosphere developed. Muhtar Kent, in the same speech, brought attention an important task is that awaits leaders of businesses, even if they are small. He spoke about and listed 2 responsibilities that leaders or CEO cannot delegate:

1. *It is the leader's responsibility to develop the company's vision in every dimension. It can't be delegated to anyone.*
2. *Provision for the development of managers who have leadership capabilities and to the planning of their careers also cannot be delegated. Right in the middle of the vision is the development of new leaders.*

Now, do you understand why I gave the definitions for real leader and nominal (in name) leader? I didn't want to enter too much into the topic of leadership, but when talking about Muhtar Kent, it's impossible not to mention leadership. At the beginning of the conversation, I said it. I mentioned that leadership is a very special topic. Now, I'd like to add this: do you understand that around us there are managers who only have the title but personally are lacking.

What does Muhtar Kent say? *"The nurturing of new leaders is at the center of a vision."*

For the love of God, are we able to see this happening neither in politics nor in the work place? Does this type of action plan exist?

– **Some companies are doing this. They are making development action plans.**
– Firstly, there is actually an entrance into your question. "Some companies" you are saying, but they are quite a few. That is few to almost none. That is the first.

The second, a large portion of those few companies are doing this on paper in order to show how much they are integrating the systems of the 21st century (in fact that the 20th century) and how they are modern companies. Because of this, Muhtar Kent is important.

He has a career journey that since the 70s has been pursued, supported and planned. And he is a Turkish-American manager. There are a few in other companies. But from what they've done I am seeing and hearing more of a "We also exist!" They don't have clear leadership development systems.

"The wise person who is able to self-rule himself is actually free."

Quintus Horatius Flaccus*

---

* Quintus Horatius Flaccus (December 8, 65 BC – November 27, 8 BC), known in the English-speaking world as Horace, was the leading Roman lyric poet during the time of Augustus (also known as Octavian).

5

WOULD YOU LIKE TO TRAVEL TO THE HORIZON?

The first key for a Journey to the horizon: don't be an ordinary person!

– **A little bit later I'd like to ask you more about our real professionals. However, at this time I'd like to change the subject a bit. I have participated in your seminars. You are always saying, "Don't be an ordinary person." Will you open this up a bit?**
– Actually, I'm not the only one saying this. This is a truth known for a long time. Here is the problem: there aren't too many people around us who are examples of this. There aren't too many different people who could be sources of inspiration for youth people or for older people as well since the value of those that do exist is not known. Yes, I will mention a few other people to you later. I will talk about those important personalities and, from my perspective, those whose importance is not yet understood well enough as well as characteristics of a leader, those that cause them to be talked about and at the same time those who are **"a real professional"**. You will see right away the aspects that diverge from classic leaders.

    I want to make a point in this regard…

    Let the upcoming generations know about these people. You will see that these people are not ordinary like the typical other professionals that we see. There is a tradition at Koç University.* Every year Rahmi Koç speaks to the graduates.

Years ago, I received from him the Vehbi Koç Scholarship Award. At that time Mr. Koç said interesting things to us. I like Rahmi Koç both as a model businessman and as a person of style, but the most important is that he is a "world person".

To like the Koç Group or to not like it is a separate topic. Its honorary president Rahmi Koç is another. Rahmi Koç has things from the four corners of the earth that he could explain to you. He is almost like a geography scholar.

Bill Gates also has a lot of money. Or George Soros. Warren Buffet also has quite a bit of money. However, they have not advocated for history, geography, antique machinery, antiques, past eras, industry, culture, and art as much as Mr. Koç has. I strongly recommend that everyone visit the Rahmi Koç Industrial Museum.

Further, Mr. Koç has a very important book called **"A World Tour with Nazenin IV".** There are many remembrances and many details. Yet from my perspective it's been overlooked. I think that the magazines didn't dwell on it too much.

Now I want to pass on to you some of the critical statements Rahmi Koç made at the Koç University graduation ceremony in

---

* Koç University is a non-profit private university in Istanbul, Turkey. It started education in temporary buildings in İstinye in 1993, and moved to its current Rumeli Feneri campus near Sarıyer in 2000. Koç University is ranked highest in Turkey according to the 2016 Times Higher Education World University Rankings. University currently consists of Colleges of Social Sciences and Humanities, Administrative Sciences and Economics, Science, Engineering, Law, Nursing and Medicine. Koç University offers 22 undergraduate, 31 graduate and 16 PhD programs. The university has about 5,500 students. It accepts international students from various countries and has an extensive network of partner-universities including University of California and other universities such as Northwestern University, Cornell University and Georgetown University. Founded in 1993, Koç University has become one of the most prestigious universities in Turkey. The University attracts many of the highest scoring students from Turkey's top high schools such as Robert College, Koç School, and Uskudar American Academy. The majority of classes (over 96%) at Koç University are taught in English (a few exceptions are found only in the School of Law and School of Nursing). (Source: Wikipedia)

June of 2010:

> *"In life, always let your words and your essence be one."*
> *"Don't be indecisive; even a wrong decision is better than indecisiveness."*
> *"Benefit from others' experiences."*
> *"In life, always be positive and seek to see the good side of everyone."*
> *"Determine a definite aim for yourself."*
> *"Don't be an ordinary person. Strive to be a different kind of person."*

As you can see these statements are open and clear. Is there any need for too much commentary? In the future, I'll come to the topic of "goal". Of course, the substance of these statements must be carried out. Did Mr. Koç carry them out?

He carried them out. And carried them out above and beyond. He was not an ordinary person. He was not an ordinary boss.

Giuseppe Mazzini* said it like this: *"Don't fall asleep in the tents that your father made. Keep pace with the advancing world."*

Rahmi Koç was not like his well-beloved father and exemplary businessman, Vehbi Koç. He changed its style and carried Koç Group forward. He did not fall asleep in the tent his father made and kept pace with the advancing world. With mistakes and good deeds, he became a world person.

---

* **Giuseppe Mazzini** (22 June 1805 – 10 March 1872) was an Italian politician, journalist and activist for the unification of Italy and spearheaded the Italian revolutionary movement. His efforts helped bring about the independent and unified Italy in place of the several separate states, many dominated by foreign powers, that existed until the 19th century. He also helped define the modern European movement for popular democracy in a republican state. Mazzini's thoughts had a very considerable influence on the Italian and European republican movements, on the Constitution of Italy, about Europeanism, and, more nuanced, on many politicians of a later period: among them, men like U.S. President Woodrow Wilson (with his Fourteen Points) and British Prime Minister David Lloyd George, but also post-colonial leaders such as Gandhi, Savarkar, Golda Meir, David Ben-Gurion, Jawaharlal Nehru and Sun Yat-sen. (Source: Wikipedia)

The second key for a journey to the horizon: to write a proper resume.

– **So, when setting out on a journey toward the horizon, in our minds will always be the wings of a windmill, and we'll put forth the effort to not be an ordinary person. At this stage, what awaits us at the second point in the journey?**
– Yes, you summarized our journey well. For one, the windmill as a symbol will always be in our minds. In that way, we won't be an ordinary person.

In order to have the life like a 5-wings windmill and even to strive in that regard in and of itself involves not being an ordinary person. Here, I also want to get this out into the open. To say to not be an ordinary person does not mean being an adventurer. In that case, it would mean misinterpreting the windmill symbolism. It's the opposite. A person who uses his/her mind, has a rich life, is not ordinary and is productive can never be adventurous. He must be a steady person. He may be different, but most of the times someone who doesn't stick his head into a problem.

After this whole philosophical but important explanation, now we can move onto boring matters. Do you know what CV means?

– **Resumé...**
– It is that, but what is the meaning of the word?

– **Hmmm. I don't know.**
– Even in the word CV, there are many profundities. Its basic usage in Latin comes from the sentence: *Curriculum vitae et studorium*. The word *curriculum* comes from the Latin verb *correre*. *Correre* passed into Italian with the same meaning. It conveys the meaning "to run, running, to quickly progress". However, *curriculum*'s exact counterpart in Italian is the word *corso*. It means "flow, distance covered, path". In this case, we can translate it like this.

Curriculum means "Corso": The Path

Vitae, and again the translation into Italian is nearly the same and means "life". Here, even better, it conveys the meaning "life's".

"*Et*" means "and".

Studorium means "studies". *Studiorium* passed into Italian as *studiare* and into English as "study".

At that, the root of the word CV is precisely this: ***Curriculum Vitae et Studorium* which means "the path (run, covered distance) of life and study"**.

– **Thank you for this comprehensive explanation. I didn't guess that it could have been this detailed. We see that it was a concept used in Rome.**

– That's exactly right. To write a resume is both a very easy as well as a difficult job. There are many reasons for this, especially since everyone's story is unique to himself.

The path that is referred to as *"corso"* is its own. When climbing a mountain, the trail that is used in particular. Some might use the opposite pathway. Respect must be shown. Unfortunately, conditions at this time have become tough. I said it earlier. I have analyzed where youth unemployment is and where it is headed.

In this sense, CV has gained a lot more importance, of course. But if we are an intelligent person, we will have needed to accept this beforehand, even if we have the most well-designed CV or resume doesn't mean anything, if the economy isn't going well, if the system has slowed, growth isn't rooted in the real sector, and growth is based on financial accounts. **In fact, this time a very qualified CV might even begin to harm you.**

There are bottlenecks in the system. **The system's valves only work from a financial /fiscal perspective. There is no valve for unemployment...**

Because the government has left the system. Workers and employees are brought into the public sector with only the mindset of fill and clear out. But there is no plan and system for development. So, then the system slows. We talked about this somewhat a little earlier. Now I am going to share with you about CV writing along with my thoughts, some things that HR managers have done in the past as well as some assertions.

– **Okay.**
– Now the situation is not like it was in the past. If young people don't have a good resume, they are eliminated at the head of the path. I want to add this as a note. In fact, sometimes a poorly prepared CV can be the reason a good education and experience can become valueless.

In this situation, those who are aware, try different paths in order to stand apart from the hundreds of other resumes. And they will try. No one can say anything to this. Some will prepare a video the length of a short film introducing themselves. Others send by cargo to HR department their work up until that day. I've read that there are even those who have sent a bagel alongside the cover letter.

– **So, what characteristics do HR managers look for and according to what do they make their evaluations?**
– For many years, I have been taking and saving notes about what some HR managers have gone through. I'm looking at what large companies have come across. I have read many interviews of HR managers. The biggest advantage of HR magazines is this: they give you tips. In this sense, I ask especially young associates to follow this perspective.

The first foundational truth that I gave was this: **be careful of knowledge pollution!**

I want to give you an example from one of the foremost telephone operators. This operator's HR department has encountered, as much news as an HR magazine, CVs in many different formats such as crosswords, a series of photographs, a PowerPoint presentation full of pictures and a presentation recorded on CD. However, when in an environment of much hiring, what they notice most is how they can arrive at the person's information in the shortest and most effective way. For managers, the important thing is that the person explains himself in a **clear and**

open way and includes core information in the format of a classic resume.

- **Workers think, "The more I write, the more successful I will appear."**
- I am saying that this is a big mistake! You need to be absolutely clear and simple. A "modern CV", in other words, means "clear" and being able to explain yourself in a simple manner.

- **What do you think of a cover letter? It's become an urban legend. It's a problem if we write them; it's a problem if we don't.**
- **Don't write a cover letter.** The period of the cover letter is now finished.

For one, neither human resources managers nor headhunters have time to read things like cover letters. We made so much noise about time management. Don't HR workers also need to manage their time? Forget reading cover letters. Companies and departments aren't able to accomplish their most basic function. When calling for an interview they are not conducting it at a certain time and place in a disciplined way. There are problems with lack of organization and standardization.

For example, let's say they didn't like you. Actually, this must be expressed in the shortest amount of time and the candidate must not be caught up in unnecessary hope. Also, the HR departments' calling of candidates who truly could make the short list it is important. In this sense, they must read CVs in a proper and clear way.

To start with, we make life harder by writing a cover letter and also creating the danger of matching the philosophies and ideas on it with the philosophies and ideas of the company. It is very hard to write a different cover letter every time and, quite frankly, is pointless. In this case, the best is to have a quality and clear resume.

In fact, Stephen Covey asserts in his book that we must go on the path with "Contribution Statement". I agree with this viewpoint. We are increasingly moving straight that way. Quite soon the classic CV will be off the agenda and the shape of modern CVs will change into the format of a "Contribution Statement".

– **Will you open to us "Contribution Statement"?**
– Every book by every writer isn't necessarily valuable. It's especially necessary to be careful with books regarding the business world. Because these books are not novels. You love a novel or you don't. This has more to do with your relationship with the author. However, business world and personal development books are not that way. It's hard to choose a real author and concept. This is why you must read a lot and be comparing as you read.

"Stephen Covey" is a writer who has a special place among the authors that I have read. His most important book is the one titled **Seven Habits of Highly Effective People**. After this one, these books also stand out: **The Eight Habit: From Effectiveness to Greatness**. There is another important work had been printed in America in 2009: **Great Work Great Career**, Stephen Covey wrote with partner Jennifer Colosimo. Here there are many tips. However, the most attention-getting theory is the "Contribution Statement". Stephen Covey asserts that everyone can have a great career. I'd like to read some paragraphs from this book. After, we can return to the CV concept.

> *"To start with, everyone can have a great career. It doesn't matter what type of work you are in. It's all in how you define a "great career". If you define it as something that brings in a large amount of money and power, it's not definite that you will be able to rise to those glorious levels.*
>
> *Of course, it's important that you have an income that you can live on, but does a great career only consist of a good salary? A person who has a great career makes an outstanding contribution and creates in others a strong feeling of faithfulness and trust. Everyone can do this, no matter the title, position or profession.*
>
> *Your special contribution is the answer you give to the "what" question of your great career. It grows out of a mixture of your unique talents and passions coming from within you. It doesn't matter what type of work you do, it's something that only you can create.*

> *Faithfulness and trust are the answers to the "how" of a great career. The fruit of your character and conscience are your greatest and best incentives. What you need to do is something that you know deep inside. How you need to do it is born out of your practice of it."*

There are much more examples like this from the book. In the end, I'm not looking at the topic as optimistically as Stephen Covey is. In short, this is what he is trying to say of the matter: Do the work that you love and press on until the end. Actually, this is what all career counselors say, however, the truth of the matter is different.

– **Aren't American writers confessing their sins a bit?**
– Exactly. That is why I approve of Stephen Covey because he became the first to confess his sins. This actually isn't a bad thing. Now, for years American writers and thinkers have written and introduced books saying, "work like this and that" or giving secrets to earn big money, 10 rules for being successful in life, or the best 20 rules for great sales, etc. They have written extremely pretentious books without actually having analyzed the system and life very well. Some of these books are good and some are terrible. But in the end, the main theme was this:

> *"If you work appropriately and learn well the 'rules of the game,' then you will be successful and in return will earn good money."*

But this didn't happen. Most of all, the "American Dream", which had been designed in that way, collapsed. People worked like crazy, but could not be saved from the spiral of debt that was created. In the meantime, some crises happened. People were crushed even more under these crises. And if it should be confessed, this system actually didn't benefit anyone. I think that the large companies didn't even benefit since every large company's selling field is different. When the consumer collapses, then the large companies also collapse. This is the main rule of the system.

I will earn so that I will spend. However, a large portion of the populace, neither in America nor in most of the developed and developing societies, were able to earn much. In fact, they got into debt. But this created a kind of atmosphere that the economy was growing. The banks gave too much credit. Why?

Because their resources were depleted. The money in their hands was imaginary. They put into circulation imaginary money, but people didn't say anything. This put the 2010s in an inextricable mood.

Since Stephen Covey is bright, he knows where this is going. And he says that everyone can have a great career. But if you forget about earning a lot of money, see that's when everything can be great. Nevertheless, now there isn't anything ask for anyway! Besides, everyone's underpinnings and stories are different. Even if everyone goes down the same road, it's not possible to arrive at the same results. A person's life and social systems are not a chemical laboratory. That's why to understand a person and to provide for his/her development, is actually like discovering " Space". The unknowns and unexpected results are one within another.

But like I said, Stephen Covey's saying that we need to create "contribution statement" in place of a CV is an important breakthrough. It is gaining attention.

Moreover, Stephen Covey, in his book describing the difference between the "Industrial Age and the Information Age", he analyzes the situation in a clear way. These are the things I appreciated the most and the aspects I agreed the most with, but here I see a component that needs to be developed. Should we read it?

> *"The difference between the Industrial Age and the Information Age...workers were treated like machines. There was what's called a "user handbook" describing the job. Just like you don't expect or want your toaster to do a unique thing to your bread, you didn't expect workers to make a unique or unexpected contribution to anything.*
>
> *But "an information worker" is the exact opposite of a machine. He chooses which issues to work on. He finds new solu-*

tions. The scope of the contributions he is able to make has no boundaries."

However, I do have some doubts. Stephen Covey does also and continues like this:

> "Of course, the Information Age is full of disorder and uncertainty. The unnerving result of the move from the Industrial Age into the Information Age is the absence of work security. As it was in the past, the possibility of having a lifetime job that guarantees a retirement salary has nearly disappeared and most likely will never return. Most of the companies on the Fortune 100 list recommend one type of pension to new workers: a 401(k) or a similar "defined contribution" plan."

As Stephen Covey pointed out, the Information Age's good aspects are great, but there are also very unfavorable aspects as well, and we need to deal with them. Mostly the Y Generation is working in the Information Age.

— Who is the "Y Generation"? It's mentioned everywhere. I know, but I'm asking if you'd explain.
— Those who were born between the years of 1980 and 1999 are called the "Y Generation". Being a bit flexible, we also see those born at the beginning of the 2000s entering the included range. The oldest of these young people are 38 and the youngest is 18 years old.

These people have differences from the previous generation. These became acquainted with computers from age 10 on. Of course, not everyone. However, in general, they became acquainted at a very young age. There are nearly none among them who do not have a Facebook account. All use social media. Their viewpoints on life are different. There have been many research studies done concerning them. Type in "Y Generation" on the internet and a ton of material and articles will show up.

They say these people don't exactly conform to the system. It's true. But don't let them forget that at one time the generation called the "Baby Boomers". WWII and those born after and the generation that brought about the events in Europe in 1968 were also a counter generation. What happened? They became a pretty good product of the system. It's as if not too much changed. They developed the system, and even if they achieved by some of the things they dreamed of, they actually were not able to accomplish expansive reformations.

– **In this situation?**
– In this situation, the information companies working with the Y Generation could move to a different model. They could establish an infrastructure that would satisfy these people. However, it's not so easy for these other sectors and structures.

Should we get to know the other generations a bit? Those born between 1961 and 1981 are called "Generation X". This is the generation I'm included in.

The "Y Generation" (Millenials) are those born at the beginning of 1980 and until the beginning of the 2000s.

"Generation Z" (Digital Natives) are those born after 2000, the new generation we are waiting for.

– **So, what are you going to say concerning Z?**
– I must give an answer with a basic logic: Did we understand "X" and "Y" so much that I should be able to explain to you Z!?

Unfortunately, we are not of those who are able to understand the social segments. Over 50% of the world's population is under 30. This generation at the same time makes up the demographic advantage of the world!! (mostly for developing countries). However, if we don't properly and scientifically educate this generation and the subsequent future one, the Z Generation, then they will turn into a demographic disadvantage (problem). Because one day these people will retire and each one will want a good retirement income.*

---

* By 2020, millennials will comprise half the global workforce: 90% of people age 15 to 24 live in developing regions where there is a scarcity of good, stable jobs. Globally, Millennials are three times more likely to be unemployed than older working-age people. For further information please visit: http://www.catalyst.org/knowledge/generations-demographic-trends-population-and-workforce

Furthermore, those born between 1925 and 1946 are called the "Traditionalists", and those born between the years 1946 and 1963 are called "Baby Boomers".

In today's world, Generation X comprises over half of the workforce in the whole world. Thus, their preferences and work life in segments called consumption, communication, etc., as well as their behaviors and expectations in their work life all differ from each other. At this point, as an additional note, it is interesting that the name of the group known as Generation Y corresponds with the English word "why?" Since in English letter "y" and the word "why?" are read in the same way.

Some authorities allege that the Y Generation was given this name because of their questioning nature. But actually, it's due to being alphabetic: "x, y, z".

– **Can we return to "Contribution Statement"?**
– Sure. Look at how Stephen Covey explains it this way:

> *"A person who is only looking for work has a resume. People who want to build a great career have a "Contribution Statement".*
>
> *You have strengths that can't be found anywhere else — you are a unique synthesis of your skills, passions, and conscience. Where do your strengths and the needs of the market intersect? Your ability to provide a unique contribution lies at that point."*

Covey speaks of 6 proper steps. I am passing these on to you briefly. Friends who are curious definitely need to buy the book. Otherwise, we'll have to quote a ton from the book.

1. *Write praise for an influential person. (Think of the most influential, effective people you know personally. Of them, pick one and write praise of that person. It could be a teacher, a coworker, a friend, a leader whom you have worked with. What contribution did that person make to your life?)*
2. *Write praise that you would like to receive. (Continued in the book)*
3. *Take a look at your strengths. (Very proper and natural. Continued in the book.)*

4. Picture your objective. *(Continued in the book. This is the point to which I give the most importance.)*
5. Develop your contribution statement rough draft. *(Continued in the book.)*
6. Share your contribution statement.

– **So, in the country in which we live, will there be an equivalent of the "Contribution Statement"?**
– That's a good question. I said something to you earlier. People like Stephen Covey determine long-term trends, because they read, these types of writers and thinkers frequently, are in contact with them and are working with a good team.

Things aren't going well in America... (for 2017-18 Economists waiting for a reasonable inflation and somewhat warm economy).

At least some of the workers can put their classic CVs to the side and move on to a contribution statement. They can write on paper as well as in the electronic world the innovation and different contributions they will bring. Without it taking hold over in the USA, to expect it to take hold in your country it's daydreaming. However, I want to say this to you, these types of practices are now coming into reality very quickly. I am thinking that this type of CV will come to the forefront quite soon.

– **I understand. So, I'd like to return to traditional CVs.**
– What did we say? There is no need for a cover letter. Outside of this, be careful with your references. References must be realistic. They must not be references who will unload. The expression, "References available upon request" can be used. This is better because "references" change with time. New managers or supervisors might come into play. Telephone numbers change frequently. Maybe it will seem funny, but some managers might not remember you as well as they did before. They forget you.

In time, everyone forgets.

Your positive characteristics don't be as up-to-date as before. In this sense, as I mentioned before, therefore **LinkedIn** is an advantageous platform. Of course, the traditional CV is a mainstay for most companies.

There are regulations for everything. But there aren't for writing a CV. However, there need to be general, valid rules, and that's what we're trying to provide.

– **The Life's Journey...** *Corso della Vita...*
– Exactly... We are explaining life's journey. Yes, they are demanding from us to be distinctive, and we will be. However, pictures are now out of fashion. We must know this.

Be careful of the picture! If it's possible, don't attach a picture. A good CV doesn't necessarily require a photograph. It's an unneeded thing and opens the way for prejudice. Also, more than one telephone number or more than one e-mail address can reduce your trustworthiness.

– **How much information should we include on a CV?**
– In general, so much information is added on to a CV that characteristics that could be distinctive are made difficult to determine in the clutter of information.

We must ask this question: **"Which information I give will bring me closer to the job for which I applied?"** This is the foundational question. As much as we are able, we need to be tangible on the resume. We need to write our project examples and what we did in the simplest but at the same time expressive tone.

People like people who appear to be expressive and strong. In fact, these people are the HR workers. This means even more. Be expressive, but not in the context of praise for yourself. You need to reflect this in a sweet and attractive way.

– **Just when I was going to ask you the question of what we need to be careful of in job interviews, you started to talk about it.**
– No need to make it into an urban legend. Two foundational parameters will be enough: **trust yourself, appear strong, and be comfortable.**

These are basically the main emotions of a job interview. In any event, it makes it easier if you know yourself and the company with which you are interacting. But there's also some barbed wire. For example, when you are meeting with different executives in every interview and each one has different personality and demeanor, these are matters that are extremely high pressure and the human factor comes into play.

– **In CVs, what other points are important?**
– Get a hold of successful people's CVs. This is one of the best methods of them all. Not too many, but obtain at the most 5 successful people's CVs and study them. But they need to be people who were raised in your country and, if possible, professionals with whom you have some common history. For example, if you are a graduate of Columbia University, then choose Columbia graduates and 5 graduates who have become very successful. You don't need to look for more examples.

Models are not actually very far from you. If you received a more humble education, then examine the resumes of professionals who have experienced the same conditions that you have. You will receive many ideas.

A little bit ago we asked the basic question here. We can add this: "What impresses HR managers even more?" Especially new graduates or candidates who will graduate?

This we can say: Those candidates looking for work who worked while in school are able to impress HR managers. An HR manager of the company that has been in the forefront fast moving consumer goods for years, a professional manager, said it like this:

> "One day a CV was presented to me. The candidate had been an intern at 11 different places and worked part-time at the same time. I was impressed by the diligence, courage, and determination of this candidate who had gone abroad for the first time with the Work and Travel program. From this young person's CV I received the message that he is of the type who will rise above the challenge of having a lot of work at once and won't cave in under pressure..."

If you notice, the message is very clear that he has the strength to rise above difficulties. Basically, this is what companies want from you. Again, the same manager says this:

> *"I advise young people to mention less of the intangibles and more of the tangibles on their resumes. For example, in place of the skills they have, it is valuable for them to mention the projects of which they are a part and what their duties and responsibilities are in those projects."*

If I'm not mistaken, Cengiz Gözükara was the HR Director of Koton stores.* Years ago he mentioned this anecdote:

> *"At the most, you are expecting promotional materials to come from boxes that come by cargo in your name. However, one day when we opened one such box, there were different examples of designs, catalogs, and brochures made by a candidate who was applying. But the most interesting thing from the surprise box was what was on the very top. It was a bagel with a note that was tucked in it that read: "My ideas are fresh like this bagel. If you serve tea, I'd like to meet you and share my ideas with you." So, we then shared it not with the candidate but with our department associates. We thanked the candidate especially for his offer and invited him to meet with us."*

Again, Mr. Cengiz said in the same interview:

> *"Gözükara, who suggests that new graduates not determine their expected income, also suggests that the numerical data such as 'I brought about 40 percent growth,' 'I'm first in sales at the store, 'I finished school in first place,' and the like are very important."*

But I believe that the first-place ranking in school as numerical data shouldn't be taken in. I don't agree with Mr. Cengiz on this matter since it can open the way to prejudice and success in school is tied to so many parameters. In some schools, teachers can cause students to lose interest in studying. What are we going to do in that case? Are we going to automatically eliminate those guys? Rather, I'm a fan of looking at the figures that come from life. And again, if I'm not mistaken, Ebru Sunal who was in

---

* http://www.koton.com/en/

human resources and the supervision of education at Vestel said this in an interview:

> "The HR Department at Vestel* gives less importance to the format of a CV but rather the contents and how the person who is applying for a job is able to express himself in the most concise way. Young people normally make their CVs long, but it specifies that is not good. It determines that an impressive resume is one that expresses well their goals and abilities.'
>
> Sunal says that a new graduate who puts forward his academic information on the CV he will prepare will appear to be more at an advantage, while the candidate with 10 years of experience is at a greater advantage by putting his work experience on his resume. "

This interview came out in HR magazines. At that time, I was collecting many clippings from magazines. For a long time, I followed the statements of HR managers. In fact, some of these I use in my seminars. Besides my own, my aim is to clearly reflect the ideas of managers in the real world.

– **Should we continue on?**
– A bank manager also said that **"the first page"** is important. The one who is the general manager assistant at a foremost bank says,

> "A resume is made attention-getting when whey uses a style of clear language and open expressions and when they include need and enough information."

Continuing:

> "I advise that the CV they prepare be short and that they express themselves in a clear way. Of course, work place experience and achieved successes will make the CV longer. However, it's important that they can express themselves openly on the **first page.**
>
> A young graduate definitely must relay achieved academic successes. Of course, while doing this, they also must state

---

* http://vestelinternational.com/

what differences this might make. Furthermore, internship experiences, as well as participation in school organizations and those outside of school, need to be mentioned. Experiences in the similar areas are also valid. The pointing out differences they created in projects and any awards and successes in their professional lives will help separate them from other candidates. The candidate's experience, goals, and preferences will be put out in the open in a way that is understood. This will help the side seeking an employee to be able to match the candidate with the position and to effectively prepare for the interview."

If you will notice, there is one important point. A CV must be short and clear. This is very strategic. Now, with all due respect, I'd like to give the name of one of our human resource managers and read an anecdote.

The CD Resume stood out...

Osman Ünal, who is now serving as Chief HR Officer at Ekol Logistics*, as many years earlier while working as the director of the HR at one of Turkey's largest construction firms, remarked that he really appreciated the cover letter of the application by a young architect in which he had summarized in a very short and clear way his career, goals, and reason that he wanted to work with them. Noting that the young man had conveyed the work that he had done up until today on a CD, Ünal says this:

> "I was very affected by way of expressing himself, especially in the visual sense. Because it was a CV that was prepared with great effort and thought and not with a "copy and paste" mentality."

Ünal says that with the help of today's technology, very creative CVs have come into his hands. There are those who send different pictures, prepare booklets, take visual introductory videos, transfer their career into pictures and apply for work through Facebook.

About all of these, Osman Ünal adds these sentences:

---

* http://www.ekol.com/en/

> *"Of course, to gain ideas you can obtain example CVs from those around you. However, let those be themselves and let them express well their goals and expectations for the future. Things like hobbies, internships, and translation which appear to be niceties but many details become meaningful when choosing. Recently, especially young people's taking part in civil society foundations and participation in social responsibility projects have become very important."*

– **How important, really, is the topic of civil society foundations?**
– Very important. Before having this conversation with you, I visited Osman Ünal in his office. He said many things to me especially about the importance of civil society projects.

Today whether it's new graduates or those who graduated years ago when we compile the differences between professional candidates and professionals, we can say that the unique factor that separates them and makes them different from one another is their civil society projects.

Civil socialists' views of work life are also different. They are people who are able to separate from the herd. They are active. They are dynamic. And to speak with them is even enjoyable, and they have many things they can explain to you.

In the past, work life didn't look at these types of things. Still many of our large and very famous firms are not able to understand this idea and don't invest in it. The way to be effective in civil society and to in fact win compassion is not to work in employer organizations or to become a member. This is very outdated.

Of course, associations like the Rotary and Lions are important. These are organizations where refined and proper people come, especially lawyers, architects, and doctors. However, these worthy organizations aren't even the civil society organizations to which I'm referring.

– **Why?**
– I'd like to add this while we are talking about the matter of CVs and resumes. Careers in civil society, a career at NGOs (Non-Gov-

ernmental Organizations), associations and foundations that do not belong to the government, to have careers in societal establishments are gradually gaining importance.

For, we are headed toward a world atmosphere that doesn't have borders. People now feel more like individuals and free. I'm speaking of civil society foundations but, of course, the real ones and the organizations that work based on **quality doctrines.** The importance of these is increasing.

– **You said "doctrine"?**
– Yes, that's it. Civil society organizations are something separate from companies and or religious organizations and sects. They are able to objectively and in an unbiased manner look at humanity and systems. This is very important.

Youth and the new generation give importance to this. Let's say that at least some of them do. Because we are talking about a large portion the societal makeup which is at the beck and call of the consumer system. However, again this type of wind is coming from the West it's ideology and doctrines through various organizations.

For example, environmentalist institutions such as Greenpeace and the World Wildlife Fund or search and rescue foundations like the AKUT Search and Rescue Association* are these types of institutions.

The important thing about these in comparison with other ordinary foundations is that what they stand for and their philosophies. In this sense, they possess critical importance. I can elucidate for you. For example, for an architect in my company, I might prefer a young person who has participated in AKUT search and rescue endeavors and still plays an active role in it. The practice he has gained over there and experience of being in a rigorous situation is important. This young person who works for hours from the dead of night until morning tells me a lot.

– **But he asks for time off a few times a year!!!?**

---

* https://www.akut.org.tr/en

– Let him ask. It's better. It must not be looked at in that way. Purely because of this people move away from civil societies. This is a very big topic. The government must work on this topic, not with antiquated association laws that blow the mind, but by working toward that which makes life easier and the development of civil society associations that possess components of true democracy. They must also work toward strengthening connections between those who take roles in these associations and their workplaces without taking advantage of them.

You will see how in the future, as for defense, health, general security, auditing, and regulation being the foundational jobs of the government, it will also be the duty of the government to encourage working at a civil society organization or even to encourage serving mandatory military service at a civil society association.

Thirty years from now young people won't be going to mandatory military service, they will serve in civil society associations. And not just men, women and men will be together. This is not a daydream. You will see that it will happen.

The government and municipalities, just like what happened with the "boy scouts" organizations, will monitor and coordinate. In fact, the government will give the first civil society association training. In this sense, I place great importance on careers in civil societies. But before this, there are some material and immaterial barriers. We must overtake these barriers.

– **Now, if we could return to the matter of the CV.**
– Yes, let's return. Now, I'm citing a manager who works at a fast-moving consumer goods (FMCG) group, *"Our managers say that most youth in order to make their CVs more impressive highlight, alongside their school information, the education they received, areas of expertise, their knowledge of foreign languages and the computer programs they use."*

He continues: *"These accouterments are very impressive. However, this shouldn't look at merely as a matter of accouterments. At the same time, it's an indicator of his desire to develop himself and of his acumen as well. Furthermore, someone who is well-equipped but anti-social has never been a preferred candidate profile. A CV complete with the message of a strong social aspect brings the candidate to the forefront."*

This manager is saying the same thing: a CV complete with the message of a strong social aspect... Like I said, I'm saying again: companies need to think a little more ambitiously and expect stronger social aspects. This is very critical.

– **In your seminars, do you distinguish according to CV types?**
– This is a universal differentiation. I'm doing it. In the traditional understanding of CVs, there are 3 types of CVs. But like I pointed out earlier, whether it's "Contribution Declaration supported Resume" method or like a CD, original CVs will be preferred more. This is very clear.

"LinkedIn" will be enough, to begin with. If you don't have a CV there, it means you are starting the match defeated, 1-0. Tomorrow if there is another platform in the place of LinkedIn, at that time we'll mention and talk about that one.

Now, CVs are divided into three categories according to their type.

Chronologic CVs...

The general technique for these CVs is this: Starting with your last job, you list your jobs going backward. You must be certain that you give the most room for your last job. I suggest that you only explain in detail your positions from the last 10 years or the last 3 or 4 positions. It will be appropriate for you to give a place on your resume to the positions at which you previously worked that have a direct relation to the position for which you are applying.

Rather than the day and month, just specify the years which were worked. You can clarify these types of details during the interview. In the end, don't forget that the CV is a serious summary of a life's run (corso della vita). A CV cannot explain you completely. It will take a lot longer time to discover you. Let the HR workers work a little to understand and discover you.

For a firm, you worked at for a long time, you don't have to specify all the positions that you held while there.

This is very important. The CVs that have come into my hands...there are friends who have worked 3 or 4 different positions at the same firm, and all of these are written out in detail. This is not correct. If you performed the same function but in different positions, instead of repeating the functions, merely explain the last position.

If you are sure of your last position and, in particular, if it lasted 2 years or more, then the best thing is to explain that position the most. In the explanations of the positions, only make room for concise and core information. Specify information especially from your last position that coordinates are relevant with the position for which you are applying.

If you graduated from university within the last 5 years, you can give the top spot to your education. If your experience needs to be in the forefront, then put the section of your resume related to education at the end. The first 5 years of your career are important. What you will endure, what is going to come about will happen during that time.

If education is strong, then it should take top place in this slot of time. But if it's not an ambitious education and experiences have encroached on education, then the education section must be moved to the bottom.

For experienced comrades who have surpassed 5 years, even if they are graduates of the Harvard School of Management, education still must be at the bottom. University is training. We know it's valuable, but now companies at that point are looking for a professional. The stages of the past serve as supporting points. They are important but not critical factors when selecting.

– **The other CV type is "functional", correct?**
– Exactly. This is actually my preferred model. It's the type of CV on which functions are more clear. Made up of 3 or 4 paragraphs that specify and briefly describe the fields in which you are an expert, this is a very clear CV.

I suggest that for every functional area, you list your successes and projects. Alongside your areas of expertise, specify and list in order of importance your characteristics that are professional or related to work (and non-related to work).

If you have graduated from university within the last 5 years then, on the top, if not, put your educational experiences at the bottom of the resume. As you can see, this rule is universal. Specify in a concise but genuine manner the workplaces, firm name, and place without neglecting the position.

– **And at last the goal-oriented CV model...**
– In order to compose a goal-oriented resume, it's necessary that you must have a definite professional job and career goal. Otherwise, this type of resume format will harm you rather than a benefit.

Your characteristics and successes definitely must be properly proportioned with your work goals and of a supportive extent. Your success and qualities must be brief and directed toward your goal. Seven or eight paragraphs may be enough. As I always say, without exaggeration, brief and concise, but powerful...

Your specified qualities must be able to precisely answer the question to what you will be able to do. As for your successes, they must be able to soundly and completely answer the question as to **what you have done up until now**. Your professional experience and education definitely have to move to the background. You need to use the very last part of the resume for this. It is enough for new graduates to write the experience you gained from your internships in the section on your qualities and successes.

> "The end of every shadow, after all, is the child of light. Only the person who has experienced light and darkness, war and peace, rise and fall, only that person has truly experienced life."
>
> Stefan Zweig*

---

* From a work titled The World of Yesterday. Stefan Zweig (November 28, 1881 – February 22, 1942) was an Austrian novelist, playwright, journalist and biographer. At the height of his literary career, in the 1920s and 1930s, he was one of the most popular writers in the world.

6

TO RIDE THE CAREER TRAIN...

– I know quite well that in your seminars titled "Riding the Career Train" you bring people to look at some sectors very closely and that you let participants know that you give importance to them and that selecting a sector is critical to one's career. Would you like to dwell on this here?

– You may have received a great education. You might know a number of foreign languages. Your strategic intelligence may be developed. But, at the same time, you need the right environment (habitat). If you dedicate yourself to occupational training in the right field, then you have chances of taking off and quickly advancing. Otherwise, professionally and career-wise your growth is stunted, and you don't have the best chances for development.

In this sense, I think it is quite appropriate for professionals to change sectors and that it necessary to support it. **It is even important as to which sector "an accountant" works in.**

– I assume there are wagons in the Career Train...
– Yes, you can think of this as a train. The machine in front of the first wagon in the train is the locomotive. That is, strength for pulling...

Power...is essential. This is that country's or eco-system's most powerful sector. This is the foundation.

– Is there a locomotive in our eco-systems?
– Yes, there are different locomotive sectors in your country that change from place to place. However, it's not easy to give a clear

answer to this question since there are 3 types of time dimensions.

The first is the dimension that comes from the past. And let's say that at this time, we see the reverberations and strengths of these sectors.

The second truth is the present time. What is happening now? At this time which sectors are advantageous?

Of course, this has 2 dimensions: the perspective of the employer and that of the employees. These are very different from each other. The matter that might be attractive for the investor and entrepreneur might not be invited to the employees.

– **Why?**
– It's very basic. The expectations and concerns for the future that the professional has do not usually run parallel with the expectations and concerns for the future that the investor has. For instance, I can give examples from the textile sector on this topic.

Occupation of my father... My father was one of the first textile engineers in Turkey. A graduate of Leeds University in England...he was going there on a Sümerbank scholarship. Studying for 8 years.

Textile is a sector that was very appropriate for Turkey and for years is one in which good money has been made. However, whether it's the rivalry with China and India or the general quick adaptation of the far eastern market, our work has come into hard times. Those who have come into the sector in the last 20 years or those who want to try usually regret it. They are not able to achieve what they want. In fact, even investors and bosses have left the sector.

The sector shrunk and, in one sense, left its spot to the automobile and construction sectors. Today we see many of those who were in textiles now in the construction sector. In the textile sector, since advancements that were made during Atatürk's time such as textile machines and textile chemistry were not combined with lateral components and strengthened. And, moreover, the added value that we had gained for years, for machine purchasing was transferred to Europe and a few other countries. Today, **"Turquality"*** and other mechanisms are very late in efforts to make **real branding.**

Of course, this isn't an easy situation. Nevertheless, I think they are late. The value-added qualities of the textile sector might be low, but people will continue to wear clothes forever. What the Italians and the Spanish could do in many fields, we were not able to do. However, even though I think we are late, I also have hope. Since it is a quick provider of employment, this sector with proper planning and incentives could return to the "magnificent" days of old. Only, you must create hundreds of prestigious brands. Otherwise, it has no importance.

– **I understand. Which dimension will we investigate? The Past, today or future?**
– Today's locomotive sectors are construction and automotive. These 2 sectors and the subsectors that service them at this time, or from another perspective, from the beginning of the 2000s have been carrying this country. That is, these 2 sectors represent the past and today. Especially automotive, in comparison with past years, has become very aggressive. It has become king in exportation.

Yes, these are locomotive sectors. However, even though we view it as a locomotive sector, "the fuel" and spare parts come in from out of the country! Only our cement, ceramic tile and iron-steel sectors aren't too bad. But I, again, know that the local value-added ratio of even these sectors is not as high as it should be or can't be due to technical reasons.

I am speaking as one who worked for many years in some of the above sectors. However, being a consultant in the career and business world can talk about the future, things will be all that much better. Of course, we must not remove ourselves from today, since the future is at future and people are not able to live in the future. They are living today. But, again, the reality is that it

---

*   http://www.turquality.com/home-page

is important now to be able to see and sense what the conditions will be **10 years later**.

In this world, the word **"to know"** is an incorrect word. **You cannot know the future, you can only predict it.** You compile data, inspirations, trends, methods of working, stances of sector leaders and information, and then you can predict the future. I am not at the head of the State Planning Organization nor do I have a position of responsibility. I am forced to make a projection. The State Planning Organization even makes decent projections, that is a separate topic.

For years, I have been following with some sectors. These are the #1 and #2 wagons, and I am listing the rest in order of importance, such as three, four, and five. The goal here to be able to open a canal for us to be able to perceive. However, in this conversation, I'm not going to widely expound on career trends. I'm only going to mention trends. The sectors I'm going to mention are those sectors in which the workers' perspective is important or could be important.

In this sense, the number one career wagon is the **healthcare sector** (It's valid for US, Japan, Canada and most of the developed countries as well).

Have you ever heard of these?

- Management and organization in hospitals
- Strategic management and planning, balanced scorecard
- Investment and financial analysis
- Unit management in the hospital
- Total quality management
- Risk management, FMEA
- Human resources in hospital management
- Patient rights
- JCI standards
- Healthcare data processing systems
- Selected topics within healthcare management
- Management of logistics and purchasing
- Expense analysis in healthcare operations

- ISO 9001 quality systems in healthcare
- Conflict management
- Communication among patients, their loved ones, and personnel
- Development of relationships among people
- Problem-solving techniques, poka-yoke
- Effective telephone communication
- Application of quality standards of service in private hospitals, evaluation of hospital performance.
- Workplace health and safety.

These are the titles of a prestigious health care certificate program. Here, the important thing is the titles and that other programs have similar contents as well. Work to examine these titles and understand them. In our region as well as the rest of the world, like USA, Canada, India, China etc. there are unbelievably unhealthy societies. And as time progresses the health of societies continues to decline. Unfortunately, if radical precautions are not taken, it will get worse.

Today in Japan, the number one problem is in the healthcare sector...

The Japanese are a people that live a long time. Of course, there isn't a young population coming up and the growth figures don't satisfy Japan. The Japanese, as if it weren't the end of the world, experienced a serious rise in population, and they encouraged this. The population ballooned and aged.

The healthcare sector is an expensive and difficult sector. Japan's public debt was already high. Suddenly forced to look after millions of elderly people, the Japanese government began to complain. This problem is very difficult for them to handle.

This is not our topic. However, I'm guessing that the least complaining ones are the Japanese state hospitals and the private hospitals. One way or another, the government is responsible for defraying the costs of the hospitals. Otherwise, the system will crash, and the country will no longer be a developed country.

– I understand...

– The healthcare sector has a few supporting legs. One of those is the government. One is the universities. Another is private hospitals. The others are labs and the medical sector. There is also the customer segment: patients, that is.

Our issue is not whether to approve of the government's implementations or not. Our issue is how the matter is being perceived. With the government at the head, the healthcare sector has begun to be seen as a company or a group of companies. This, in essence, is a good thing. But of course, if you can operate providing rights and finding the right staff. Or you must adapt to the current staff, but this actually where work starts to become difficult.

We have too many soldiers and police (in most of the developed and developing countries). There are a fair number of lawyers. Teachers are in abundance. In fact, there are thousands waiting at the door to be brought on staff.

But what isn't there? There are no **healthcare managers**, but where is the potential for growth? In the healthcare systems!

Here, for example, is a shortfall of expert doctors. This shortfall has especially grown in recent times. Because the number of hospitals has risen, the number of family doctors, as well as projects such as a doctor for nearly every block or similar regulation changes have greatly increased the need for doctors. And it will continue to cause it to increase.

Look... Whether it's poor nutrition, the using the wrong oil or sedentariness...because of these types of problems, just like in the United States of America, the biggest problem is the weight problem. If I'm not mistaken, in recent years the combined overweight or obese adult population has reached 64.9 percent (for Turkey). This is the Health Ministry's formal data.

Let's say that half of these 64.9 percent are obese or have a high potential for becoming obese. This figure is even high. Today in Europe and America this issue has almost become the first item on the agenda.

In the end, whether we separate sources of preventative medicine and diet systems, this sector, whether we like it or not, is going to grow due to numbers of unhealthy people. In this case, there's a shortfall of two kinds of worker shortfalls: **medical shortfall and operational shortfall.**

I recommend all young people studying in high school if they are able to be even-tempered and brave enough to not escape an intense and long education, to consider the profession of being a **doctor.**

However, if they say, "No, I can't study that long or become that fatigued, but I still want to be in the important sector of healthcare." Then I recommend they receive an education in **"Healthcare Systems Management".** Even if they are going to be in human resources manager, I recommend they become a **"Health Care Human Resources Manager".** Here the employee openings will be numerous, and, in time, there will be a great need for many human resource managers who know quality healthcare personnel.

Furthermore, like I said, you should find the institutions in your country, who are giving serious training on this topic. This training, in my opinion, is more important than many MBAs or master's degrees. You know how when we talked about the suggestions for how you can be a real professional, we talked about the importance of specialization. And at that time, I talked about the **CISSP** certificate program. You should find an appropriate healthcare development program in your city, state or country.

Also, sub-disciplines such as **"Health Law"** will also be strengthened in time. The concepts of law problems in the health sector, doctor's rights and patient's rights will become more established. I have also come across programs in this area in some law schools. But it's worth contemplating especially for law students.

Have you ever heard of these issues?

Medical ethics, criminal liability of health workers, medical mistakes from the standpoint of medical ethics, malpractice, aspects of law and malpractice, complications and expert witness implementation, organ transplantation ethics and law, reproductive law, rights of doctors regarding service, etc. There are many sub-disciplines. There's a lot of bread and butter here. It's being made known to the young people.

– **It's also effective as medical tourism.**
– That's exactly right. Today in the world, there are approximately 100 billion dollars spent in medical tourism. I think this figure will greatly increase in the future. Just like in the example of Japan, as the population ages health problems will increase, more people will become ill, and this will create more tourist activity. The basic factor here is medical quality*.

Medical tourism, alternative tourism systems such as cultural tourism, golf tourism, and congress tourism systems must be on the rise. Especially, the young generations must focus on the alternative service sectors, not the conventional ones.

– **Okay, at this stage, would you briefly mention the other trend wagons on the career train?**
– Of course, like I said earlier, I am going to give you a critical list. I'd love it if you publish this list.

- Energy sector (alternative energy, green energy, renewable energy)
- Data processing sector (computer engineering and every type of software development specialization, internet and server systems specializations, risk management)
- Telecommunications sector (communications engineering, fiber optic systems, internet communications)
- Academics and consultancy (in some fields)
- Defense industry
- Management of music organizations
- Aviation systems and management
- Art/exhibition/museum organization and management
- Railway systems engineering
- International law
- Environmental law

---

* The Turkish expert doctors are great. Turkish doctors are provided with good opportunities and are well-equipped and they are well-trained mostly.

- Sports law
- Health law
- Specialization in digital and social media systems and specialization in interactive advertising systems
- Architecture and interior design, sub-specialization in designing every type of comfortable and secure building and space
- Normal and luxury yacht production
- Marina operation and management
- Gastronomies and restaurant management (in the upper bracket, high-class segment)
- Nanotechnology implementation in medicine and in all fields
- Physical therapy
- Psychology and Psychiatry
- Recreation specialization
- Private finance consulting (money and other assets)

These and other systems make up the new wagons of the career train. **This train is not an ordinary train.** This train is the fastest train at this time. Either you are inside this train, or the another cog in the wheel of the system. This is a critical decision.

Some of these will need 5 years to become more active. Others, however, will need more time. I must say this: a critical factor in success here is tied to your governmental bodies (the country where you live). We will seize onto the systems of the 21st century to the degree that your capital city wants it and according to how seriously and accurately they provide direction. Otherwise, unfortunately, we will have a very difficult time.

– **This must be the difference between the past and today. In the past, there weren't these many disciplines and specialization had not gone this far. Don't all of these new divisions and new systems make the job harder?**
– Bravo. Exactly! Of course, it makes things harder. This is the issue.

Today in all over the world when you ask companies this question: "Are you able to find the employee calibrated the way you want, with the characteristics you desire?" you come across an interesting (and actually a situation I'm not sure which word to use to characterize) situation.

They say "No, we can't find them. We have a qualified worker problem." When asked in which fields, they say they aren't able to find well-trained workers in technical areas. Also, they are saying that there is a problem with unskilled labor. They can't find enough unskilled workers. Let's ask the same question of firms such as Google, Apple, and Coke and see what answer they will give!

At this point, I'm explaining the difference between these companies and the others. What brings these companies to the forefront is the importance they give to human resources and to the **humanitarian index**. However, sadly I must say that today in large companies there are also problems. Quality is not at the forefront as it was before. I am saying this looking at the observations I have made in life and the overall concessions in quality that have been made.

– **Quality was important in the 90s, wasn't it?**
– Yes, the 90s were interesting years for developing countries mostly. They were years of awakening for companies. Yes, maybe banks were being poorly managed but somehow bank workers were more content than in the 2010s and 2000s. Banks overall might have been not doing well, but they were giving hope from a career perspective.

Today, the banks have set right their balance sheets, have developed one way or another and have brought their monetary funds to a strong position. But wait one minute! Are the bank workers happier? Are they earning more compared with the 90s? Can they easily climb the career ladder? Is it prestigious to be a banker? Or is it only good and enjoyable if you are at the head of the bank?

In fact, at the top, there are very severe winds. The truth is that there are in every sector. But bankers are on the edge of the precipice. Of course, I'm not talking about state banks. Their style of management, organization, and structures have always been different. To be a worker in a state bank above all meant to be a government employee. To a degree, it's still that way.

Now banking has stopped being attractive. We can say it's become fatigued. As I've said, of course, I'm not talking about the top management at some banks. Because they earn a lot and they always can come by new opportunities. Today, even if there aren't as many banks opening, even so, when a new bank does open, to whom will they give the first offer? To the upper-level managers of other existing banks. Even if the transfer money isn't as much as before, they are able to receive it as well. However, if I'm not mistaken, in the past even middle-level managers were receiving transfer wages. When referring to white-collar workers bankers were coming to people's minds. Today, no matter which banker I talk with, he is unbelievably disgruntled with his life.

– **Isn't this a contradiction?**
– Yes, very much a contradiction.

The critical factor became this: after living through the last crises, especially the 2001/2008 crisis, it became a perfect touchstone. After the banks came under the control of oversight boards and were groomed by them, the system itself began to degrade. During the crisis thousands of experienced bankers became unemployed. It became cheap to return them to work and this did away with the strength to the bargain of those who came behind.

Some of the banks went under. They closed. But it meant that the situation for the banks that remained was better. Furthermore, most of the countries were forced to implement a hot money policy (especially BRIC countries including Turkey). The government, which in the past had implemented high-interest rates, in order to protect itself and to reduce its own debts encouraged the private sector to take on debt.

The private sector became more and more in debt. Banks obtained many syndication credits. Nevertheless, as you know, most of these debts were with foreign currency. In this situation, the value of the foreign currency shouldn't increase too much since these debts will be repaid.

What did the banks do with the money they obtained? Of course, they didn't distribute it to the middle and lower level workers as a nice gesture or bonus. Banks, in principle, did the right thing and disbursed it as a credit to the people and to companies. However, much it isn't exactly accepted, there are also problems with credits. Not all are sound, and actually can't be. I am seeing that foreclosures have increased by a lot. The consumer credits are especially problematic. In other words, it has not gone to the production systems but rather to the consumption systems (especially in developing countries).

– **What do you want to say?**
– I need to say this. What was our topic? Career train. However, this is no longer a bank wagon on this train. And I suppose there won't be one for a while.

– **Quite assertive, isn't it?**
– Banks will lose its importance in this system. However, upper-level banking will be more important. Financial advisors will be crucial. In banking one of the components that will be important is "security systems".

– **Security systems?**
– Yes, remember those experts who received the CISSP certificate that I mentioned in our previous conversation... The importance of experts like them will increase.

Look, most of the money that is held in banks is virtual. Money is flowing virtually from one place to another. Millions, billions change hands every day. The balance sheets that are made are even virtual. It is also easy for manipulation to happen in this system. Or to intervene with the system and cause it to collapse or to open the way for big mistakes.

Because of this, banks that have large networks have to protect their servers, that is their stored information. They must be well-protected against hackers and other attacks such as viruses and evil-intentioned credit card number copying.

In the future, there won't be too many branch offices. Banks speedily and noisily are trying to get internet banking to catch on. I am very curious about money that is spent in this area. I suppose that IT security budgets have long increased 10-fold the traditional in-house training budgets.

Internet banking along with another kind of consultancy will be on the forefront: **finance consultancy...**

Finance counselors are the old brokers, bankers or bankers who don't want to work for the establishment. In fact, special exams and certificate programs will appear related to this matter. These people will check on your investments from where they sit in their homes. Your money will continue to stay in your bank account, but you will give "advisor intervention authority".

They along with the banks will collaborate to perform transactions and will manage your money according to your risk perception. They will send you weekly and monthly reports. In fact, these people will keep track of some of your special payments, your owed taxes and other of your financial obligations. Different financial advisors will take on the work of stock market brokers, bank authorities and financial assistance services.

Today there are already similar experts. These are using their authority to carry out different financial trade transactions using the banks' screen. I think that development of the system I described is for the benefit of the banks. Already, banks provide service for an "A class" customers under the heading of "Private Banking". However, I am talking about a service that is much more less costly and reaches a much wider audience; its coverage is much broader and is a new type of expertise.

You will simply have a counselor in a monetary sense. These advisers will come into play in the next phase when buying real estate, a car, when calculating a car's depreciation, or even when paying title deed fees. The provision of this service can't be avoided. I'm awaiting it with excitement. There are similar examples in America. I'll talk about them later.

* * *

"Water hollows out the stone, not through force but through persistence."

A Latin Adage

* * *

– **I suppose you're not going to talk about the other wagons on the career train at this time!**
– Yes, I don't want to talk much more about these wagons in our conversation. Since you asked and it is wondered about quite a bit, I talked mostly about the healthcare sector. I preferred to give brief information about the other sectors and trends. At another available time, we can have a more comprehensive conversation about these topics, and I think we can give our followers more information.

– **OK lastly, in this sense, if we were to make a projection, which disciplines will be in the forefront?**
– Of which professional disciplines are we talking? For example, if I say to you, "go and be a singer," am I saying to sing in the nightclubs? Or if you are beautiful and well-proportioned, am I saying to go and be a model? Or to our laborer friends, am I saying, "There will be a great need. Go and work for a cleaning company?" In security systems, there is a large shortfall. I'm not saying that you must be a security worker, am I?

It's not because I look down on them. Never. I have an incredible amount of respect for every type labor. However, the labor and career paths are different from one another. Actually, everyone is a laborer: white-collar or blue-collar... Everyone is a worker in exchange for money, for wages. However, there is a nuance. This must be understood.

I am claiming that a security worker can have a career. This is only possible under certain conditions. The company worked for and the system must be open to this. You could make your way up to security management or even the general manager of a security company. This is possible.

I say that friends who work in daily wage professions, temporary work such as modeling, manning a booth or a counter or those who work in the service sector can move to a professional discipline (way, path) where they also can have a career. I'm saying that they need to try. Let them try at least a few times in their lives.

Like what Stephen Covey said, **"Be proactive."** For a **"great career"** you must play well. And very well. This is a big revolution. In this sense, I have always had greater respect for this type of career.

At this stage, we can divide the groups of professions into 6 basic classifications:

A. Temporary, daily wage jobs
B. Services group or technical support group professions (gray-collar, intermediate worker, intermediate professions, intermediary services)
C. Blue-collar workers
D. Green collar workers (workers in the green energy sector and technical team)
E. Collarless (information industry workers)
F. Lasting and long-term professions in which other doors can be opened up to you (some white collar workers)

– **Now, are you saying that everyone should be directed to long-term professions?**
– No, of course not everyone can do lasting and profound work. And shouldn't do it. This is contrary to nature. However, know this quite well if you have a place in groups A and B or you aren't a white-collar worker with a sound/valid profession; if you are a white-collar worker who has a profession that isn't effective; and also, particularly if you are working in the service sector, especially, those working in this sector. From a long-term perspective, this group of the profession doesn't have many guarantees. In addition, not everyone needs to have a career. But no matter what, concerns about the future will develop.

– **So, what should they do?**
– In the first place, it's good for them to experience concerns about the future. Normally, worrying isn't recommended, but what did we say at the beginning? If worry and hopelessness come together, then fears develop and creates problems.

But I recommend, even if it's just a bit, that the friends in the 6 groups that I listed earlier thoroughly worry about their decision. Of course, I'm not talking about a worry that will trigger depression. There must be some **professional development concerns in us.** We must ask this question: "What will my professional development be?"

Everyone might not have a super, quality and profound profession. Not everyone can be an electronic engineer. Not everyone can be a medical specialist.

But what did we say earlier? For example, if you believe that the healthcare sector is going well, at least is not going to go under and that it's a respectable sector, if you also are a blue-collar worker in this sector or a gray-collar, it means you are in the right place.

Furthermore, you can develop yourself and be in contact with institutions that teach "Healthcare Management Systems", or you can receive advice from doctors and health care workers that you are able to trust. It's not as hard as it used to be to work toward an associate degree, and when finished you can receive a certificate. It's not an impossibility.

Of course, healthcare systems aren't the only sector. There are many different disciplines. A little earlier we mentioned some promising sectors. **Aviation** for example. It's a field that is very active and up-and-coming. Also, any type of work with the **railroad systems** will be attractive. The engineers who will work in this discipline will be at a premium and so on. The workers in other divisions of this sector will be at a premium.

Don't ever give up. **We don't even give up when dying. We have hope that we will go to heaven.** Isn't it that way? I'll come to the topic of motivation and goal-making. However, like I said, the friends working in the A, B and C professional collar groups need to work more and do more research. They need to come out of the cave.

They need to participate in many seminars, watch videos by consultants and read articles and books. This will broaden their horizons. Of course, your journey toward the horizon will have costs. The biggest price to be paid is that of setting aside time for these things.

If someone says, "No, I am happy with my condition. I will retire in this same way. I don't have a problem. I am very happy." then it means there is no problem. Our words are for the unhappy and unsatisfied anyway.

– **I understand. What about the USA?**
– Moreover, I must say this: the trends in the world and the trends in the United States are somewhat similar. However, the "career development" and "career analyzation" is done more frequently and much better in America. The unemployment problem is researched even more. Why?

Because America is a very large country, and its problems are big. In this sense, there is a need to frequently analyze and follow the trends. Furthermore, despite all their problems, it is a very developed country. In general, it's a rational country. Of course, despite this, they aren't able to get on top of their problems, but that's a separate topic.

You asked what's going on in America...

"The Best Jobs in America" list is put out by "cnnmoney.com" every year. The 2012 list was put out, but I notice rather than 2011 is an indicator of the first 10 years. That's why we can consider this list as a projection until 2021. This research concentrates on 20 professional disciplines with the most marked developed and makes a different analysis of them. I'm going to list the 10 professional disciplines with most marked development.*

---

* http://money.cnn.com/pf/best-jobs/ (the site updated the list and they are serving currently only the years of 2012-13-14-15-17 please look for latest developments from the link.)

Now I must say this: we can't say that the developing world definitely mimic America 10 years later in every matter and every field. However, in financial systems and also especially in the information field, we, by and large, imitate them. This is true in some of the healthcare trends, treatments, and engineering fields.

OK now, let's look at America's top fields for last 10 years (and probably next 10 years):

Software Developers: In America, this professional discipline grew 32 percent in the last 10 years. For years, I have been explaining this professional discipline in my seminars. Even though this is a professional discipline that is developing a lot and is desired in developing world, its importance is still is not fully understood. I can say that it is the most critical profession. In the 21st century, these workers will be the most requested and needed workers. Their work will be a near guarantee. The best part is that they will need to continually develop themselves. Of course, since this is a profession that involves a lot of sitting, these experts need to balance things out by participating in lots of sports! Otherwise, it's a profession that can open the way to serious impairment.

Physiotherapy: We talked about the importance of the healthcare sector for developed and developing countries world. In countries like America and Turkey, where the population is quickly growing and actually isn't very healthy or in countries like Turkey, India, Iran, Middle East etc. where there are frequent traffic accidents, it is very smart to become an expert physical therapist or physiotherapist. It's a very strategic profession because the developing sports world has a great need for this profession. There will be a demand in this field until a significant pileup happens. Of course, I'm not talking about uneducated physiotherapists. I'm talking about good and scientifically educated physiotherapists. Today, even "Pilates" instructors earn good money. You can expect physiotherapists in hospitals, hot spring bath complexes, sports clubs, universities and physical treatment centers to work in a more disciplined fashion and to earn more money.

Regardless, their importance in the system is going to increase since there is a trend regarding this topic in America as we saw and in the world. Rather than physical exercise, we see that physiotherapists receiving an intensive and rigorous education have become the trend. Of the components that will be coming to "developing world" from America, one of them could be the increasing importance of physiotherapists.

– I understand. I'd like to return to "financial consulting". Would you expound on this a bit?
– A financial consulting in America has rather taken the form of an individual's turning to a one-on-one counselor. It's someone who is asked for methods to make the most out of money. In the CNNMoney survey that I mentioned a little bit earlier, **financial consulting** comes in 3rd place. In the last 10 years, it grew 30 percent.

It's a model that has been used more by banks and insurance companies. **However, as you remember my model that has much more extensive coverage than these types of analysts.** In this sense, I'm thinking that, whether in a narrow or wide range, this occupational group is going to develop in the next 10 years ahead of us.

The financial counselors in the USA gain this title by passing a 10-hour gigantic exam. Furthermore, those who have worked in a related field for 3 years are being sought. These systems need to, first of all, be established in emerging markets too.

Civil Engineering takes the 4th spot in America. In the first 10 years of the 2000s, it grew 24 percent. I don't to make too many comments, but, not only in America, it's true that it's a profession that has a universal rising and is always a respected profession.

In 5th place is **Marketing Specialization**. In America being a marketing expert is always attractive work. Partly in the 80s but rather more in the 90s and up until the beginning of the 2000s it was a desirable field. The marketing departments worked like the manager grooming departments did. However, from my perspective, it's lost its old magic.

– Why? Isn't marketing important at every stage? Marketing is marketing. Isn't it important to sell merchandise in every period?

– Yes, it's very important, and from this perspective, you are very right. Nevertheless, don't forget this: today the way of marketing has changed along with the speed that mobile devices have brought and the development of internet-based social media. Now traditional marketing methods of the past are not valid. Especially if we talk about fast-moving consumer goods and confectionary products.

In the past, there were the classic **"4 P's"** of marketing. These were abbreviations of English words and was especially modeled by "Phillip Kotler". This model was sold to the world. Let's recall these 4 Ps if you want. What were they?

– **I suppose he said: product, price, place, and promotion.**
– That's exactly right. If you'll notice, these factors still stand. However, of these factors for long-time marketing managers have not been able to reckon with the **price factor**.

Of course, they can give their ideas, however, pricing is in the control of sales, finance and general managers. In this sense, I have been saying from the beginning that marketing hasn't been able to be done properly.

Secondly, the expectations of the youth and people of this age are very different. Now classic promotion and publicity activities aren't that attractive to people. To explain and show to them on television how superior the products are that you are presenting isn't as appealing as in the past. Now the product's classic description has changed. The answers that were given to the question, "What is the product?" all of the components that made up the product were given.

However, now there is an asymmetric understanding of a product due to social media and all the millions of signals that are thrown at us. People have figured out that the concepts that marketing has thrown out such as Mother's Day, Father's Day, New Year's Day, Valentine's Day actually artificial and, in reality, are a tactic of marketers. Or at least I'd like to think that way.

This has taken marketing out of the attractive area of the past. Also, in the past, it was a larger field and strategic. Now "New Marketing" or "Social Marketing" concepts need to be looked at. Have you ever heard of the concept of **"Subliminal Message"**?

– Is it something in psychology?
– Yes, Mr. Sefer Darıcı employed as an academician wrote a book on this topic: **"Subliminal Invasion"**.*

It's a fabulous book. I think everyone should read it. Mr. Darıcı summed up this topic well. He explains with examples. There is a marketing world that attacks us using commercials, television series, placards and all its systems.

They use "smell". Even the smell that you experience as you enter a shopping mall is important. It must be a smell that drags you to consumption and shopping. The colors that are used are unbelievably important. The colors in a store. For example, the launching color of a new model car. Or other alternative colors.

The design of logos and colors and other visual components. The use of sex and sexuality. You can understand it's a journey in the subconscious.

Look, there's a lot of information stored here. We are talking now about something way beyond marketing. You must know well the science of psychology and systems that rule the subconscious. Normally you would expect these courses to be in universities, but they aren't. At least I haven't heard of them.

Over the course of time, two more **"P's"** have been added to marketing. These are "People" and "Process and Process Management". At this, it became the **"6 P's"** Here the word "people" is not referring to customers. It refers to human resources. Actually, Philip Kotler and previous scientists at that time were passed over, but actually, he was the most important figure. The

---

* http://www.idefix.com/Kitap/Subliminal-Isgal/Sefer-Darici/Egitim-Basvuru/Psikoloji-Bilimi/urunno=0000000418752

"real professionals" that we described and the right people need to be the marketers.

Being a marketer requires a creative culture and to almost be a social scientist.

In the case of **"Process"**, there's a whole continuum. The completion of the process of goods reaching the customer. Procedures, dominance on the product tree, procedures for brand development or as for an independent system even settling on a name. In the end, no matter what it must have a very good archive and database. It's expected that the marketing departments and marketers overlook their own processes as well as all the processes of dealing with agencies until the launch of the product.

– **I'm assuming you are saying this isn't enough!**
– Actually, to place marketing into a mold is a big mistake: 4P, 5P, 6P or 14Ps.

These brief and clear defining expressions were invented by the American academic world to **"market marketing"**. They are strategic abbreviations. To reduce it to the basic and to make it much more understandable. It's a marketing tactic.

Philip Kotler and that movement implemented this very well. However, not staying within my limits, taking inspiration from Sefer Darıcı's very well-modeled "subliminal message" which is the issue of the subconscious message, I'd like to bring a **7th P** to marketing: **Psychology.**

Psychology is field that is in every, and I mean every area; appears in front of us at every opportunity; one in which the understanding and application of it are very difficult; one that has too many variables due to the human factor being a part; and thanks to even economic systems is an extraordinary field subject to change. If you don't know psychology, you can't do marketing.

– **But agencies don't already know this?**
– Of course, they know, but not in an orderly way, I'm thinking. I'm assuming they've not delved too deep into it. They are being

managed by people who have received very little psychology training. Or they don't have a concept of it.

Whether it's in companies that I've worked in or those in which my friends have worked, I've not heard of or seen the marketers and salespeople receiving psychology training! If there are, let them speak up. I'm curious. Also, you said it well: Agencies.

Actually, agencies are doing a large part of the work that marketing departments normally should be doing. There are agencies that are extremely professional and do their work well. So, they have a go at it. If the initial idea comes from the marketing people then they develop and carry out the campaigns and all the dynamics. It falls to the marketers to approve or to give the final word. In one hand, I see this as normal, but large companies absolutely must have very strong marketing departments, not mediocre.

In fact, not just national, but we have a need for departments and professionals who know well, can develop and implement international marketing, a concept which we have quite neglected.

– **What would you like to say regarding international marketing and export management?**
– Look, a country is developed if their "professional exporters" are the country's most resplendent white-collar workers or, to put it differently, earn good money, are affluent, and from the car, they drive and all the way to their lifestyle are the highest-level professionals.

If those exporters are going to represent their country's brand in the international arena in the best way, they will sit on the most prestigious chairs in the company. Everyone works to imitate them. They try to learn the foreign languages that they know. They try to understand the international style of life. This is a great thing. A little while later these prestigious professionals, since they have high motivation, cause their countries to earn more money and make their brands shine.

Exportation is a difficult profession, just as being a doctor is. But unfortunately, in most countries, this world went full-throttle in the 80s but stayed there. Just when we were going to move from connection-based to marketing-based, the internet came and muddied the waters. Everyone assumed they could be a "professional exporter". Bosses put their sons and daughters at the heads of these jobs just because they knew foreign languages. I'm not criticizing this situation. If your neighbor does it like this, if this became a normal thing to do, then every boss does it. Also, I think that from now on exportation shouldn't be called "exportation", we should say "international marketing". I'd like to see this breakthrough in the system. Until this happens, unfortunately, I am not able to explain my own profession of exportation as a wagon on the "Career Train".

"Advertising is a valuable economic factor because it is the cheapest way of selling goods, particularly if the goods are worthless."

Sinclair Lewis*

---

* Harry Sinclair Lewis (February 7, 1885 – January 10, 1951), better known as Sinclair Lewis, was an American novelist, short-story writer, and playwright. In 1930, he became the first writer from the United States to receive the Nobel Prize in Literature, which was awarded "for his vigorous and graphic art of description and his ability to create, with wit and humor, new types of characters". His works are known for their insightful and critical views of American capitalism and materialism between the wars. He is also respected for his strong characterizations of modern working women. H. L. Mencken wrote of him, "If there was ever a novelist among us with an authentic call to the trade ... it is this red-haired tornado from the Minnesota wilds." He has been honored by the U.S. Postal Service with a postage stamp in the Great Americans series. (Source: Wikipedia)

* * *

"Ads are the cave art of the twentieth century."

Marshall McLuhan*

– **So, then I would again like to ask about a career in marketing. Under the circumstances, a marketing career isn't that grand, right?**
– Now, if I say this, your young friends might become discouraged. Today if you go to universities and take a survey, nearly 60 percent will tell you that they do want a marketing career. However, this is very wrong.

Neither the universities nor the companies are able to accurately give direction to young people. The problem here actually springs from the foundation. Poor planning and too many schools of Economy and Administrative Sciences. For the stu-

---

* Herbert Marshall McLuhan, CC (July 21, 1911 – December 31, 1980) was a Canadian professor, philosopher, and public intellectual. His work is viewed as one of the cornerstones of the study of media theory, as well as having practical applications in the advertising and television industries. He was educated at the University of Manitoba and the University of Cambridge; he began his teaching career as a Professor of English at several universities in the U.S. and Canada before moving to the University of Toronto, where he remained for the rest of his life. McLuhan is known for coining the expression "the medium is the message" and the term "global village", and for predicting the "World Wide Web" almost thirty years before it was invented. He was a fixture in media discourse in the late 1960s, though his influence began to wane in the early 1970s. In the years after his death, he continued to be a controversial figure in academic circles. With the arrival of the internet, however, interest has renewed in his work and perspective. (Source: Wikipedia)

dents, the field that appears the most reasonable and attractive seem to be marketing and sales, especially marketing.

– **Why?**
– It's very simple. It is a refined field. That's why.

– **So, comfortable?**
– No, comfort is something else. Rather than comfort, like I said, it's a "refined" professional discipline. Generally, in this discipline, you have contact with upper-level people. Those you interact with are agencies and the upper-level management in a company or sales organizations. Normally rather than from sales, there is a responsible supervisor from marketing. You either interact with them or with the assistant general manager above them as well as with the general manager. They don't really enter into the market. You don't have to have contact with the less-educated. In this sense, it's a refined field.

– **Could we say removed from the general public?**
– This changes according to the place, country, company and culture. But marketers don't prefer to be in with the general populace and consumers. Of course, this leads to their not being successful in the long-run.

What did we say? In our conversation titled "A Real Professional's Main Truths" ...at the head of a professional's most basic truths are relationship management and social intelligence. Not only marketers but all professionals need to meet frequently with the public, with consumers and, in the end, with customers whether active or potential candidates.

– **Also, there's also loving and embracing the product you market? Isn't that right?**
– I'm always saying that there is no room in your work life for the word "love". Especially women workers refer to this a lot. When I ask them why they want to do this work or are doing it, they say to me that **they love it**.

Actually, in work life there needs to be, not love, but **to understand, to know and to embrace**. First, you are going to know a product, a professional discipline or a company and its culture, later you will understand it. You need to make this profession or function that you have understood your own.

After internalizing all of these, now you must believe in that profession and function, culture, product and even the company where you work. But this belief should never be blind faith. We are talking about appropriating and faith in the professional sense. This "faith and appropriation" at the same time needs to be done in an enjoyable environment.

You can say that you really enjoy doing a job or selling or marketing a product. But to say, "I love" isn't a good thing.

Love, a healthy love, can be toward a person, an animal or a thing. I love trees a lot. I love nature. I love Michael and Gabriella. I love my girlfriend. But I can't love my work. I must be an open professional who can leave his work tomorrow. In love, there is no walking away that easily.

Work life is done expecting reciprocation and if possible while earning good money. It must be done this way. Please don't enter that profession without understanding this and not experiencing the steps, at the very least in your mind.

– **In brief, this is what you are saying: "Don't market a product you don't believe in."**
– Yes, "to not love", the right word and philosophy is "to believe". This is an important component of "career philosophy". You can't love a job, a profession. I'm saying it again. You can love a woman, a man, a color, a piece of music or a flower. Career life doesn't rest on love but on the words **"belief", "appropriation"** and **"enjoyment".** Let's use these words.

– **Then, marketing is a good career, right? Your last word?**
– Before, I gave you a list. I said "Wagons of the Career Train." There are some sectors on it. It might be interesting, in those sectors is to do marketing, but believing and appropriating marketing. You need to analyze that and think on it.

Marketing is always a good discipline, but like I said, there's a pileup. In order for you to get into a good and quality marketing department of a company. You need some very special conditions and chances. At this stage, I don't want to go any deeper.

– Do we want to finish the other professions on the list?
– Of course, in 6th place is **"Manager Consulting"**. In America, it grew 24 percent in the last 10 years. This profession is interesting and needs to be dwelt on.

"Manager consultants" are consultants who give support from outside without a place on the management board, helping whether the bosses want to go with the flow of cash or information regarding economic systems and other forecasts. In this sense, we should wish good luck to those who want to pursue this line of work. But ten years later we can see some of its implementations in emerging markets too.

"Information Technologies Consulting" comes in at 7th place.

If you notice, people in America who generate ideas are in an appealing situation or increasingly desirable status. This professional discipline grew 20 percent in the last ten years. In the same way, this is how CNNMoney explained it:

> *"Of the areas in which firms have made the most investment at the top is technology. Recently, due to the increased need for mobile devices and applications, the demand for those (consultants) with expertise in information technologies is increasing."*

Number 8 in rank is **"Management of Data Systems"**. You know the certificate system that we talked about earlier, CISSP. This area is where those who have certificates in this program and one like it "Information Security" can work. I highly recommend it. In America, it grew by 20 percent in the last ten years and generated an average yearly income of 86,600 dollars. Some data systems specialists received 120,000 dollars a year. This figure is important.

In 9th place is **"Financial Analyst"**. This is a very classic field and is in increasing demand everywhere in the world. However, one I didn't recommend but is very attractive is in the **"operational economy"**.

– **What does that mean?**
– I will explain it at the end of our conversation.* In 10th place is **"Environmental Engineering"**. In the last 10 years in America, its development was 10 percent. However, the reason it's 10th is that a whole 50,000 engineers entered work in this field.

One survey says that the increase in the importance of such topics as the best way to use natural resources, protection of the natural environment and the development appropriate to human health have caused the demand for environmental engineers to increase. However, **environmentalism** is mostly a governmental policy, a life philosophy. People cannot be environmentalists by themselves. They must be trained, made aware, and feel the need.

However, in very developed countries such as Germany, there is the "Green Party", and these determine public opinion. They are considered to be very powerful. At least they are not weak. But in that country, there is a very broad education system and thanks to a strong higher-learning system and there's a large conscientious population. In these types of countries, there is an **"environmentalist"** understanding.

In the past, this was not widespread in America. However, America knows that it really polluted the environment, and regulations and implementations in this regard are increasing. The environmental engineer employment may have increased in America, in this sense.**

---

*   Please look for details at additional sections of the book.
** After Trump, these regulations and implementations can become weaker and the environmentalists movement in USA can have some drawbacks.

"The desire to understand the world and the desire to reform it are the two great engines of progress, without them human society would stand still or retrogress."

Bertrand Russell

7

WHAT IS REAL POWER?

– I'd like to touch on more real professionals and I want to know more some of them. However, now I do want to hear from you the concept that you have explained in your seminars called "real power". I'm thinking that without understanding real power, we cannot fully understand what it means to be a real professional.

– Yes, I think you intervened at the right time. I was going to talk about a few more "real professionals", but this is good.

If you attempt to implement the 3 basic truths without understanding real power then you can't even start moving. What is this strength?

The concept that I call "real power" brings together the many psychological, personal (skills), societal, emotional, logical, divine and rational factors into a **motivational strength and strategic intelligence.**

Actually, the "windmill" illustration that I mentioned earlier, real power is the wind that turns the windmill. Without the wind, the windmill doesn't turn and actually is worthless, isn't it? Of course, the main strength of the motor is Almighty God. Without the skills and energy that Almighty God gave to us some of our characteristics wouldn't be present, right?

This "real power" that is made up of all the factors I mentioned above is needed by everyone. For a farmer, for a soldier, for a government employee and for a manager in any field...

Since without the real power the 3 main truths that we listed earlier, without energy, it will come to mean that this actually not a sustainable performance and that it cannot answer the question of why we need to be real professionals.

In my required soldier duty, I was a third lieutenant infantryman. While serving as an officer in the Bitlis 6th Armored Brigade the motto that I saw on nearly every wall comes to mind. In fact, I also hung it on a wall. It goes like this:

- Pursuit ✓✓
- Control ✓✓
- Coordination ✓✓✓
- Motivation ✓✓✓✓

Each of these was starred. Each was very critical factors for success. Truly with these 4 principles you can save lives or achieve great successes.

Pursuit is important, in this sense it's 1 star. Control is 2 stars, meaning it's a more important concept. Coordination is a must, marked with 3 stars. Motivation, however, is a 4-star concept.

No matter how much you prepare, prepare. No matter how good your technic is, let it be. You must be motivated. This is the essence of work.

– **Just like great scientists or sports people, right?**
– Exactly. Whoever of the great scientists you look at, look and see that they were tied to the aim, I'm calling this **"goal-consciousness"** that they believed in with unbelievable motivational strength.*

For example Leonardo Da Vinci he is described as an incredible genius. He definitely was a genius. In fact, when explaining the term of "genius" we use Leonardo Da Vinci.

Why? Because he was unbelievably intelligent? No, what made him great was his very great ambition, desire and motivational strength. Intelligence by itself doesn't express anything. Now everyone knows this and is saying it. With motivational

---

* From 20th Century Albert Einstein life is very good example to have goal-consciousness character; please watch the famous tv series: http://channel.nationalgeographic.com/genius/

strength, the windmill begins to turn. Leonardo's goal-consciousness very high.

Do you know what the methods are that Leonardo Da Vinci developed?

– **I know there are a few principles...**
– In 2000, a famous speaker and thinker Michael Gelb wrote a book: **How to think like Leonardo Da Vinci: Seven Steps to Genius Every Day.** Furthermore, for Michael Gelb's extremely influential writings and essays, I recommend this site: michaelgelb.com.

So, what are these principles? In order:

1. Curiosita' (In Italian it means to be curious): It's tied to not being able to get enough out of life along with wonder and learning. It requires learning without discriminating against any topic or discipline, not pulling back because of what those around us will think or say, to ask without losing interest and to research.
2. Dimostrazione (showing, proving): means to test the information through trial, the desire to learn from lessons with determination. Everything that is learned definitely needs to be tested through trying, then its accuracy can be decided.
3. Sensazione (emotion): means viewing emotions as a vehicle in life experiences that continually need to be refined. We need to listen to music, draw pictures, go to museums, taste different foods and drinks and touch everything around us.
4. Sfumato (evaporated, passing from one color tone to another, hazy): ambiguity, it means the desire to embrace instability and paradox. In order to be successful in the developing world, we must become used to working under ambiguities. Keeping our peace when faced with a paradox, we can have an effective and healthy mind. This is very important. It's at the forefront of what we want to see in real professionals.

5. Arte/Scienza (Art/Science): Science along with art, has the meaning of the development of the balance between logic and imagination. Every person possesses all kinds of capabilities at birth. To these I can add this: some of us in some areas have more ability than others.
6. Corporalita' (concerning the body, the flesh): For success, a person first must be at peace with himself. One factor that will provide this is to have a healthy, graceful and balanced body. For this, a person must develop the physical structure that he possesses. For the purpose of achieving this, a person must stay away from stress, keep a cheerful mentality, eat a balanced diet, have an orderly sleep schedule, keep in mind refinement and protect his health.
7. Connesione (relation): means to understand, evaluate and think systematically about the relationship of everything with the whole. Briefly, to work to understand all of our experiences and their relationships with one another. We must evaluate it all together.

– **The principles you have described are like a reflection.**
– Exactly. The path of your mind is one. I am explaining with the "windmill".

Michael Gelb also, using the 7 principles above, summarized very well his investigations Leonardo Da Vinci's life and what he's done. While our followers should do these. My 5 wings windmill model or these 7 principles aren't all there is. **They need to find their own realities, their own truths. They need to try to do this.** This is actually what we are expressing.

Do you know when you are able to take professionalism to the highest level? **When you have tried a lot and made many mistakes.**

– **We mentioned motivation...**
– What is the basic factor that makes up motivation?

– **In your seminars, you are saying to trust yourself.**

– That's it. The characteristic of being able to trust yourself is a must. First people will trust themselves and then will take steps in a sensible fashion. The professional that I mentioned earlier: Muhtar Kent and the professionals that I will mention later Ali Nasuh Mahruki, Professor Onur Güntürkün, Dr. Rıza Kadılar, Professor Mehmet Öz (Doctor OZ), the gardener who looks after the lawn in an exceptional manner, a doorman of an apartment building, a student, a teacher or someone with religious duties, no matter who they are, they need to **"trust themselves"**.

– **Can you describe trust in oneself?**
– Trusting yourself is to use your mind with absolute belief and trust and for doing works that are grand and give pride!

Should I continue? I am saying that as long as you don't trust yourself or believe in your strength you can never be successful and happy! Otherwise, the way is opened for your hopes to be dashed because your feelings of inferiority and inadequacy, but if you trust yourself, you can achieve success!

To continually think on positive things develops your sense of trust in yourself, and no matter the difficulties, it ensures you're surpassing them and for your strength to not wane.

What did Rahmi Koç* say? Let's recall!

"If you trust in yourself, you will see great forces coming to your aid."

This might look like a classic statement. No one will come to the aid of someone who is standing still. You will desire, you will trust in yourself and you will stand firm. You will see people and all around you coming to help you in one way or another. This is not the universe or anything. It's not like the crazy notion of the pull of the universe.

People love those who trust themselves. It's that simple. When you gain the sense of trust in yourself you provide your beliefs with power, you dispel your fears and you see your feelings of insecurity disappear!

---

* https://www.forbes.com/profile/mustafa-rahmi-koc/

I'm saying to fill your minds with belief and a sense of trust in yourself. These will drive out all your feelings of doubt and insecurity.

– **So, we trusted in ourselves and our motivations has begun to rise. You are saying that what influences motivation is "goal-consciousness". Apparently, there are differences from classic goals.**
– Precisely. They are very different. To begin with, it's good if your goal mustn't be an ordinary goal. Of course, being ordinariness and extraordinariness is relative.

Something that looks very ordinary to me might look amazing to you. However, again it needs to be said that it's a generally valid goal. For example, a caretaker at an apartment building can never please everyone. This is a very classic situation. But if 80 percent of the people are satisfied with you in an apartment building like mine where there are 36 apartments, then I think it's all good. Our apartment building caretaker, Hussein, is this type of employee, and absolutely professional. His motivation is complete. He is a real professional.

Recently, Hussein underwent a very serious heart surgery. But not much, one month later he was again outside working, and a little bit later was pulling weeds in the garden and was taking care of the building.

Hussein's "Frankl Grade" isn't bad...

– **What does that mean?**
– Have you heard of Viktor Frankl? An Austrian...

Viktor Frankl is the founder of the **"Logotherapy"**. Accepted alongside Freud as one of the most important psychiatrists, the "Frankl Grade" is related to giving **meaning to life.** Does what degree do you explain the meaning of your life?

People who are high on the **Frankl Grade**, in general, are driven, orderly and know how to give meaning to life. Those people are special. Like Gandhi and Mustafa Kemal Atatürk, the common characteristic of all great leaders is that their Frankl Grade is at the highest point.

They don't complain. They do and they make it happen. **Look, everything can be taken out of a person's hands except one thing. The result of the freedom that a person can have is the characteristic of choosing one's attitude under any kind of condition. You cannot take away from someone the characteristic of being able to choose an attitude.**

The Frankl Grade is for measuring how conscious and responsible we are. In later conversations, I'd like to speak more on this topic. However, the highly goal-oriented professionals that I explained naturally have a high Frankl Grade.

If we're to return to the topic, the amount motivations grow with the size of the goal. **In this sense, as much as is possible, you must choose a goal is appropriate to your system and your capabilities.**

If we need to generalize, you will work as eagerly as your goal is **"grand"** and **meaningful.** This is universal. **It isn't determined by how much you are going to work nor by how healthy and strong you are. It's determined by how earnest you are! What increases desire is the meaningfulness and grandness of the goal!**

The grandest and most meaningful goal is the one that encompasses your life! Your grand (meaningful) goal is your star that will shine your whole life. Please pay attention to what I said last.

What we are calling a goal is dynamic. It's not passive. It can show some variability according to the time and the place. **This is goal-consciousness.** While on your way to the grand goal according to the time and the place, the intervention tactic that you are going to employ is goal-consciousness. Furthermore, today what you do, or even your smallest preference, must have a connection to your greatest goal.

It's just as important that every little goal support and be on the same path as the large (grand) goal. If you'll notice, in this sense our time management models and goal-consciousness correspond with each other. A real professional, in any case, is someone who uses time well. In that sense to be goal-minded means that you manage your time well out of necessity. It means that you are advancing on the path toward being a real professional.

– **But not everyone's goal can be grand...**
– Everyone can have a grand goal. Everyone has big goals according to his perspective and environment. It's not important that your goals be materially grand. Even if your goal is small from a material perspective, it can still be a meaningful goal.

Then the goal in a spiritual sense becomes a grand goal. In fact, this type of goal is a more enjoyable and most likely a healthier goal from a physical and spiritual health perspective than the material goal.

For example, if you don't have a house, it's a goal to own a house, isn't it? Also, it's a smart goal. Because it will save you from having to pay rent. For many people, this is quite a large goal. This is material goal setting.

Furthermore, don't you have spiritual goals, or your career, your health or even managing your weight? Sometimes these can appear to be "very large".

Maybe your **grand goal** is to drink your tea in your home comfortably. This can be very significant to some people. To be able to drink your tea comfortably and without concern in that house. To be able to make this happen most of the time it's not so easy. Actually, in the background, it can have a lot of significance and might be a grand goal.

– **How are we going to go forward?**
– You must increase your goal and place all your goals in the right places under your largest goal! Not everyone will be on the top. Not everyone will be a CEO. That will only be one person at each company. This must not be forgotten. But whoever wants to be bigger, he will be higher!

However high you want to be, you will be all that much closer to the top. This is true for our work lives, social lives, sports lives and our intellectual lives. Desire the heights...**YOU desire...**

This mustn't be forgotten: most of the time the effort we will spend on little (material and spiritual) goals is not less than the effort we will spend on large and meaningful goals. When you reach the large goals, the pleasure and enjoyment usually take away the tiredness from your effort.

Meaningless and ordinary goals (material and spiritual) rather try your spirit and might open the way for your suffering. This opens the way for your skills to atrophy over time. So then why should we strive, right? You strive, but later remember the words of **Aziz Nesin** that I relayed at the beginning.

– **There will be motivation, and you are talking about an absolute belief as well. Can you elaborate?**
– Earlier we talked about an emotion the matter of "love and believe".

To embrace. This is absolute belief. Let's love (or not) a profession or a job. This isn't that important. But actually, we must **believe.** This is the essential word and emotion. **You can never be successful at something you don't believe in. I want to say this.**

However, much you strengthen your level of certainty in a skill, the effort needed for it will decrease to the same degree. If you are confident nothing is impossible. However much you believe you will succeed, the possibility that you will succeed will be all that much. By the way, a belief must be a real one. Not just a word!

– **You're saying that to believe is half the journey.**
– I'm not sure whether it's half the journey or the whole! But I do know one thing! **The strength of your belief determines the strength of your spirit.** You come to a place where you can do the same work with that much less effort, environmental factors rush to your aid and your fate is determined by the extent of your desires.

I know this. I've experienced it in my own life. This has materialized in many of my friends' lives and in the lives of the professionals that I am going to mention.

> "You may delay, but time will not."
>
> Benjamin Franklin*

---

* **Benjamin Franklin** (January 17, 1706 – April 17, 1790) was one of the Founding Fathers of the United States. Franklin was a renowned polymath and a leading author, printer, political theorist, politician, freemason, postmaster, scientist, inventor, civic activist, statesman, and diplomat. As a scientist, he was a major figure in the American Enlightenment and the history of physics for his discoveries and theories regarding electricity. As an inventor, he is known for the lightning rod, bifocals, and the Franklin stove, among other inventions. He facilitated many civic organizations, including Philadelphia's fire department and the University of Pennsylvania, an Ivy League institution. (Source: Wikipedia)

– **What role does strategy play in goal-consciousness? You mentioned the cooperation of motivation and strategy for real power.**
– To determine strategy is to find the answer to the question, "How can I reach my goal?" I can say that to know how it will be done makes up 80 percent of your ability to do it. You need to determine with all certainty the turns on the paths you are going to take.

Exactly what, how, where, when and how much do you want to do? Have you determined your goals? If you don't know exactly what you want, you have not right to object when what you didn't want is given. A planned goal is one that was all the details and steps that will be taken starting with today and on into the future are established.

– **You talk about a pyramid. You touched on it in a previous conversation.**
– Yes. This must be part of a hierarchal system. You must be able to place goals inside a pyramid. The most concrete and general goals must be at the top of the pyramid. You regard this as the biggest goal. This is your life's ultimate goal.

I'd like to give an example from my life.

In university, I wanted to study International Relations. There was no desire to be a diplomat or have any job in the public sector. My purpose was to be an exporter in the full sense, like having the ability to do international marketing.

I wanted to do this at a large and important firm before entering my 30s. This was my meaningful and big goal. According to it, I determined my comprehension of my efforts and tactics. In keeping with my ultimate goal, I took many steps from age 18 until 29, and at age 29 I became the foreign sales coordinator of Brisa (Bridgestone Corporation and Sabancı Tyre manufacturing company).

Moreover, there was a required two-year military duty period between my ages 26-27. It's possible to see this from some perspectives as a win or as a loss. Now it's which side you look at the glass. However, if it's close to a 2-year required military duty, then that means it could be before 30. I proved this to myself. After that then you can make other goals or not. In the end, I reached my goals consciously using tactical attacks and, of course, by working hard.

– **In order to develop our strategic systems, is there a book or resource you can recommend?**
– If you'll notice, for nearly every subject heading or system I'm giving a relevant book or website address.

For this topic, I'll mention one book. For those readers reading this talk, if I want, I could give much more book references. But that wouldn't be right. It would just confuse them. Furthermore, the books must be basic, understandable and clear.

There's a book called **Thinking Strategically.** I recommend this book. It's a publication of the Harvard Business School and the writer is **David Collins.** David Collins is a professor in the Strategy unit at the Harvard Business School. He is an expert in company strategy and universal competition. He provides consulting for many large and important American companies. This book, Thinking Strategically, explains it in only 111 pages.

It is a booklet but is very comprehensive. You can find anything you want in this book.

If you combine what I have explained and motivational strength with what is explained in this book, **"real power"** will emerge.

– **I understand. So, what kind of method should be practiced?**
– For the last 10 years, I have been using the "mind mapping".

It's an extremely effective method. Today, I have taught this method to dozens of my clients and many have used it. If you discover this method and experience its benefits, you can arrive at extremely productive results.

Your goals or what you are going to do must be written every time and in every way. We don't have much of a writing culture in our lives. I think this is one of our greatest deficiencies.

A person who reads loves to write. Since we don't read, we don't like to write. Most particularly to draw! It takes a whole lot of hard work. On this topic, Tony Buzan is the living legend in this world.

Tony Buzan has many books regarding this mapping technique. Of these, I especially recommend two of them. I think that these books can explain to our readers who read them what I'm wanting to say.

Don't ever do mind mapping on the computer, because this isn't something that can be done on the computer. You absolutely must draw on an A3 notebook held sideways, and while drawing definitely uses colored pencils.

Tony Buzan's books **Mental Toughness** and **The Power of Creative Intelligence** are important. I highly recommend them. "The Power of Creative Intelligence" in some ways is a more compact and clear book. Now I'd like to give an example from a page of this book:

> *Great Geniuses and Notetaking*
>
> *When you are starting to create a mind map, taking creative steps into the disciplines in this way by bringing your thoughts into an observable state, you will be joining the group of the great geniuses who used the basic components of the mind mapping.*
>
> *Among these geniuses are Leonardo Da Vinci who was chosen the "Mind of the last Millenium;" the great sculptor and painter, Michelangelo; the famous biologist Charles Darwin; the one who discovered the law of gravity Isaac Newton; the discoverer of the theory of relativity Albert Einstein; the famous political leader and writer, Winston Churchill; the one who changed the face of the 20th century, Pablo Picasso; English thinker and poet, William Blake; the inventor of the elec-*

tric light bulb, Thomas Edison; the one who with his views on the topic of astronomy began a new era, Galileo; Nobel Prize winner chemist and radiologist, Marie Curie; and famous dancer and choreographer, Martha Graham.

You're in the right place! A great many people think that the Italian Renaissance materialized due to creative genius' escape from the prison of linear thinking. These geniuses not only brought their thoughts and ideas into view with lines of text and words, but at the same time, and in fact, in a stronger way, they did it with the language of images, drawings, diagrams, codes, symbols, and graphics.

– **Not everyone can be a genius!**
– I'm not talking about everyone being a genius. Just the opposite, we are copying the methods of the geniuses. Today if we could build our educational system with mind mapping, believe me, we would have a very different society in 10 years.

– **The tablet and computers are of interest at the present time.**
– In our day, you can't work without a computer. On the other hand, this is where we are mistaken: if you immediately give a computer to people that are not developed **aurally, visually,**

cognitively and physically, the results will not be good.

There definitely must be computer education, but the computer needs to be used as a supporting unit. A student definitely must play an instrument.

Playing an instrument increases an individual capacity. At the same time, also from a social aspect, it's very valuable, just like playing sports. In order to fulfill **the 5-wings of the windmill** that we have modeled, a good education is very helpful. Otherwise, we struggle when using our intelligence and our potential. This also ultimately boxes us in.

Even if we are at least very successful in a few areas, in the end, we aren't saved from unhappiness.

– **What can you say about the development of creative intelligence?**
– Again, I want to return to the book, The Power of Creative Intelligence. On page 32 Tony Buzan mentions 10 basic methods for our doing creative work. I don't want to read all of them in detail. I want our readers to especially get this book to read it.

So, what are they?

1. When examining your life use all of your mind's abilities. (He's referring to the use of the right and left the side of our brains. Michael Gelb explained in his book that Leonardo Da Vinci developed this system. It was principle number 6, Corporalita.')
2. Education (balanced education for ourselves and for our children).
3. Take Breaks.

I want to relay this section to you since it's very important:

Surprisingly, if in the full sense, you want to be creative, thinking with your whole brain, you need to take regular breaks.

Think: where are you when you've experienced an explosion of your imaginative strength, you've found solutions to problems or you've fantasized and imagined? Most people gave these answers:

- *in the bathroom*
- *in the shower*
- *walking in the country*
- *before falling asleep*
- *on a walk*
- *listening to music*
- *driving on a long road*
- *running*
- *swimming*
- *lying on the beach*
- *goofing off*

   In these times in what state was your body and mind?

   Calm and relaxed.

   In these times of relaxation, the 2 sides of the body are in communication with each other and chat. A large portion of your creativeness is known as having the facility to express yourself.

   . . .

If you are insisting on continuing a lifestyle where the left side of your brain is under pressure, your brain will bring have a hard time letting you take a break. From the loss of concentration to minor breakdowns, different situations are possible. You can become a bad-tempered and angry person. The only way to treat it is to relax and unwind!

Do this consciously. Make your mind and yourself take a break. Your creative intelligence will love this.
Let's continue:

- Go on long walks. This is what the Romans called **"Solvitas Perambulum"**. It's a technic to increase your coordination skills while walking and "solve while walking."
- Be creative in your daily life.
- Establish your mind group and your heroes.
- Use both sides of your body.
- Take colored notes of the "language of the mind".

– **In this case, we will have to read these books...**
– I highly recommend them. In this life of ours, two books aren't that much, right?

* * *

"Persistence needs patience, patience needs time."

Alper KUL

* * *

– **In your seminars, you are "persistently" mention being "persistent" and "brave". Does being persistent always mean being brave?**
– Of course, it's not. I explained it earlier.

We must never lose the filter of the mind. First, we will be **smart**. We will make our calculations. Then we will make a decision.

But now once a decision is made, we must follow through with it to the end. The end is apparent. There are two. Either you will be successful or you will be unsuccessful.

This is a good thing. At least we know what will come to us in the end. Here the critical point is that whether it's with success or with the lack of success, we will know how much of a hit we suffer and how much of a price we pay. We will definitely pay a price.

However, this amount mustn't be above what we can overcome.

Look, every success by its very nature if isn't supported by new success or new steps then it carries the risk of being forgotten and lost. This is a characteristic of the evolution. However, from this don't think "development craziness".

I'm not saying let's put everything aside and only be successful. We were already talking about how the 5-wings windmill system is not a one-sided development but 5-sided. This must be received as basic.

– **You mean certainty...**
– Yes, if you aren't sure of the course of your actions, then don't go in.

Let's say I want to learn Italian. I am very eager in this area. I have some doubts. What are these doubts? In order to learn Italian, I must work for three years. During this three years, what else do I need to do? This is the first question...

The second question at this time is how much money am I going to spend and how satisfied will I be with the education that I'm going to receive? Do I need to go to Italy and stay for six months? Let's say that I gave my 3 years, and I learned a lot of Italian. Great. Now how will this information benefit me?

– **"One language, one person. Two languages, two people." Don't many languages mean many people?**
– That was in the past.

No more now. In our day now the only advantageous thing is learning the languages of cultures where the alphabet is different, their economic systems are good, they are doing a huge amount of trade and they travel as a tourist.

What are these? The Russian and Arab languages.

– **Chinese?**

– No, I don't put Chinese completely in this category. The Chinese are mostly pragmatic people. Even if they don't learn English well, at least they support learning it. Because in this way, they will sell goods, produce and export. But this is not true of Russians and Arabs. In recent years, the desire to learn English increased a lot. From what I understand, Russians spent a lot of money investing in it. But I still think they have a long way to go. The Arab world isn't tidy. There is every type of Arab sub-culture. Due to this, learning Arabic is advantageous in some respects.

Let's go on to our topic.

For instance, Italian. When making a decision under these conditions, in the end, I want to ask this:

Where is Italy going? Do Italian companies give priority to those in your country who knows Italian? Can I earn money from this effort? Or is mine a romantic ambition?

All of these questions enter into strategic thinking, and when you are able to answer them, it increases your **level of certainty.** This makes you successful. If you are certain, you need to stick with it.

Just like in the Italian example, even if it's not fabulous, you need to work to be able to communicate at a decent level. Otherwise, don't begin. It will be bad. Time will be lost.

– **I get it...**

– Don't forget this: **timidity, hesitancies, doubts**...all of these feelings and thoughts whittle away at you. *Timidity is dangerous.*

I am always saying this in my seminars: **Everyone admires the brave, no one respects the timid.**

And...

"The inescapable cost of giving up is a lack of success. The only reason for the lack of success is giving up."

You mentioned "persistence". **To be persistent...**is an unbelievable strength.

Do you know what the main influence of persistence is?

The main effect of persistence is not with your actions, it's the outcome of your actions. One aspect of your persistence is connected to your deep consciousness. You are persistent by continuing to think and act.

Look, persistence is primarily mental persistence. For as long as persistence is in you, it will continue to direct all of your attitudes and actions. As long as you don't give up and change your mind, your spirit and deep consciousness will continue to be influential on your behalf. "Persistence needs patience. Patience needs time."

– **And you're saying to wait for the best...**
– Yes, to wait for the best.

I want to read the headings from my seminars...

- ✓ If you hope for the best, you will definitely succeed in reaching the best.
- ✓ If you wait for the best of something, a great strength develops in your mind, and best begins to come straight to you.
- ✓ In this way, the creative strength within you comes out, and this strength causes you to concentrate on your desired goal.

I am saying to give yourself entirely to what you want to obtain.

If a person gives himself entirely and concentrates on it, he will overcome all of the barriers that appear before him and obtains what he wanted to obtain. It's that simple.

And lastly, I'd like to definitely add these sentences: If you put your whole self into a difficulty, and if you direct all your strength to overcome it, that difficulty will be broken to pieces and will disappear.

In life, for you to be successful and to reach the key to the feeling of absolute satisfaction at the horizon, then you need to desire from the heart to reach the good end of the work you do and give yourself with your whole self to that work.

8

THE REAL PROFESSIONALS

– Okay, so again, I'd like to return to "real professionals". You mentioned that you'd like to give more examples on this topic. Frankly, I am curious about the details of some of the people that you mentioned in your seminars. For example, you mentioned Dr. Oz. Why Dr. Oz? You had already given the example of Muhtar Kent in the world of business. Does it help to give the second example?

– We have very valuable academicians, doctors, engineers, lawyers, and businessmen.

We have many people in the service sector.

But as I explain this, I'm noticing this. Which barriers have these people overcome? What have they experienced? And also, I'm especially explaining the real professionals that have international characteristics who can be examples to every person.

These people are able to establish very clear and successful relationships not only with their own people but with the four corners of the world which mean each one has earned the right to be a more powerful example.

Moreover, a waiter friend at the restaurant you go to today could represent a real professional too. **He could come to you as a "real professional" with his quality service, smiling face, good knowledge of the work, using his time well along with other characteristics. You could come across them at any place.**

For example, that pilot who knows his work well. That cabin employee. That cook. That bellboy. He is our worker friend.

That person might make mistakes. In fact, might make large mistakes. But their demeanor and methods are clear. Their goals are apparent. As long as their ethical stances are not corrupted, great and true professionals are made by making mistakes and losing. Don't forget this.

– In future conversations can you give examples of these people as well?
– Yes, I'm thinking. We can give examples from every sector and every discipline. However, we are going to give priority to those real professionals who have shown themselves in the international arena.

At this time, the other real professional I'd like to mention is Professor Mehmet Oz. Actually, everyone knows Mehmet Öz as **"Dr. Oz"**.*

Compared to the other professionals, he is one who has set himself apart in the area of communication in recent years and has become a very well-known medical professional with his extremely successful television program in both America and abroad.

And he is not just a cardiac doctor. At the same time, he is a **communications professor!**

So much so that he is a communicator who has caused the whole world to be in awe of him. Whether it's in medicine or whatever discipline it is in, part of my theory is the one must have very good communication management and social intelligence, we see this rule very well especially in Mehmet Oz.

I don't want to go into too much information about Professor Mehmet Oz. It will be enough to give his CV. I want those who aren't familiar with him to know who he is. There are many resources on the internet, but I'd like to give his biography that I liked on Wikipedia so that it can be a resource that is independent and doesn't allow commentary. I suggest that those who know English go to this resource's formal address that I bene-

---

* https://www.google.com.tr/search?q=mehmet+oz&source=lnms&tbm=isch&sa=X&ved=0ahUKEwjamP_BwOrTAhXhJJoKHRlJCosQ_AUICigB&biw=1366&bih=662

fited from and am going to give: http://blog.doctoroz.com/author/mehmet-oz

Mehmet Oz *(born June 11, 1960, Cleveland) Turkish-American physician and presenter.*

He is a vice president and surgery professor at Columbia University. He manages the Cardiovascular Institute and Complementary Medicine Program.

On June 11, 1960, Mehmet Oz was born in Cleveland where his father was working. He graduated from Harvard University. He is known for his fields of clinical specialty in minimally invasive cardiac surgery, mitral and aortic valve surgery, adult heart transfers, mechanical heart implementation, coronary bypass and aneurysm surgery. He is involved in research regarding minimally invasive cardiac surgery, complementary medicine, analysis of health results and artificial heart prosthetics.

As Mr. Career, one of the magazines that I pay most attention to, the economy magazine Forbes, chose Mehmet Oz as 2011 the 3rd most influential person.

He was chosen by Hippocrates magazine as "Doctor of the Year",

By Healthy Living magazine as the "Healer of the Millenium",

By New York magazine as "The Year's Best Doctor",

And by the World Economic Forum in Davos as "Tomorrow's Global Leader".

As well, he was chosen as "The Turkish-American of the Year" in 1996.

Mehmet Oz was mentioned in the Castle Connolly Almanac and has received many awards.

His book "For Healing from the Heart" was worthy of the Books for a Better America Award.

He won the Robert E Gross Research Scholarship (AATS, 1994-96), Mehmet Oz, who has the "American Society for Laser Medicine and Surgery Research" prize also received the Blake More Research Award from Department of Doctors and Surgeons at Columbia University.

A member of many professional associations and establishments, Mehmet Oz served on the board of directors for the American Board of Thoracic Surgery (2004) and American Board of Surgery (1992).

I want to add one more piece of information. Just like the other real professionals, Dr. Mehmet Oz gives a lot of importance to civil society efforts. He's not just a member. He enters into management and actively works on the administrative councils.

Let's move on...

He is married to Lisa Oz and has 4 children named Daphne Nur, Anabella Sezen, Zoe Yasemin and Oliver Mustafa.

The television programs on which he has participated and personally hosted:

- "The Second Opinion with Dr. Oz" on Discovery Health
- "Life Line" on Discovery Health
- "Daily Rounds" on Discovery Health
- "The Truth about Food" on Discovery Health
- "Live Transplant" on Discovery Health
- "National Body Challenge" on Discovery Health
- "You: On A Diet" on Discovery Health
- "Ask Dr. Oz" The Oprah Winfrey Show
- "Dr. Oz Show"

Furthermore, other than this biography, I'd like to open up a parenthesis about one of his children. One of his children, Daphne Nur Öz, is a perfect relationship management expert, just like her father. She participates in television shows. The book she wrote was very influential in America: **The Dorm Room Diet.** You can obtain more details information about Daphne Nur Oz on her official website: daphneoz.com.

There are sympathetic explanations of diet systems on the "The Chew" program on channel ABC. Over there a team and Daphne Oz together do very good work: http://abc.go.com/shows/the-chew/cast

Dr. Mehmet Öz* has millions of people who follow him. You could be one of them: facebook.com/droz

---

* Dr. Mehmet C. Oz, the Director of the Cardiovascular Institute at New-York-Presbyterian/Columbia University Medical Center in New York City, discusses results from the PARTNER study. In the study, surgeons compared the results of minimally-invasive Transcatheter Aortic Valve Replacement procedures to open surgeries in treating patients with aortic stenosis (narrowing of the aortic heart valve). To watch please:

https://www.youtube.com/watch?v=w0Xm2LtPTec&%3BHD=1%3Brel%3D0%3Bshowinfo%3D0

And please visit also his official Columbia University web page:

http://columbiasurgery.org/mehmet-c-oz-md-facs

And small nice anectode:

http://columbiasurgery.org/news/2013/08/22/keep-calm-and-carry-youre-doing-it-says-mehmet-oz

At this time, without going into too much detail, I'd like to mention to you more people on my list.

– **I understand. True. I suppose at this time we've come to the another important real professional...**
– That's right. What I was going to say at the end, should I say at the beginning?

– **Sure! Why not?**
– linkedin.com/in/rizakadilar/

Please, may everyone visit this address and understand what I'm wanting to say.

Dr. Rıza Kadılar is an amazing personality. In my opinion, he is someone who has become a little excessive in some points. It's true that he is not a normal professional. He has a resume that is active to an ultrasonic degree and exhausting. A little bit later we will read his formal resume. True expertise in banking...

However, this aside, upon seeing what kind of communicator he is, people will be amazed. Dr. Rıza Kadılar is an amazing communicator and civil society participant.

Just before doing this interview with you, I personally visited Dr. Rıza Kadılar in the company where he is currently in management. I had an approximately 40-minute meeting with him, and I came away from this interview having learned a lot of things. For example, I am someone who is curious about the energy sector, but I only have basic information on this topic. I visited him in February of 2013. He mentioned to me a system that was not well known at that time, **shale gas**. He said that thanks to this discovery or, more accurately, technic, the American economy has a chance to recovered (actually is true after several years, the oil barrel stabilized around 50 USD due to shale gas technology).

We talked about other topics in addition to this and signed a book that I enjoyed reading, **Carbon: An Opportunity or a Threat?**

I knew Dr. Rıza Kadılar better from both economy magazines and the statements he has made concerning the energy market. During my visit, I had the opportunity to get to know him better.

He is explaining himself very well at his official web site. I'd especially like to bring attention to his steps toward and successes in **specialization, communication, and social intelligence**:

"*I was born in 1968 in Ankara.*

I studied at the AÖD Tevfik Fikret High School and at the Ankara Science High School. I completed my university education in the Industrial Engineering department at ODTU. I received my Masters in Economics at Stanford University, my MBA at HEC, and received my doctorate in Communications from Marmara University.

A while after plunging into the work world, I completed that Strategic Bank Management program under the organization of INSEAD Executive Education and put into practice some academic efforts (TBB Publications) alongside my banking career.

I began my professional career at TEB* and was in administration in various areas. In 1998, I went to Holland in order to establish TEB's first foreign partnership. After continuing my career at TEB NV as the bank's Turkish representative, at the end of 2002, I became the representative of the general manager at the London-based Sabancı Bank, PLC. The reconfiguration of the structure of Akbank organization resulted in my appointment as the general manager of a Holland-based bank, connected to the group as a foreign partnership. Afterward, I joined one of Europe's most foremost investment banks, the France-based Natixis, as the country manager of Turkey. I was also serving as Turkey's representative in the international consulting firm Pramex International which is within the structure of the group.

I am married and the father of one child.

My coaching and education profile:

---

* https://www.teb.com.tr/en/

Subsequent to my doctoral work, I began my education career in the framework of an international association, Junior Chamber International (JCI). I have taught for this association, which in general has the highest-level educator in the world, since 1999 with the title ITF (International Training Fellow), heavily focusing on personal development in European countries.

I educate on the topics of Personal Brand, Leadership, and Networking.

As the head educator of the JCI Leadership Academy, during the years 1998-2006 I contributed to the development of over 600 young people coming from every European country on the topic of leadership. In the training that I gave under the structure of JCI, I was able to reach over 3000 participants from nearly 20 countries.

In the subsequent years, I also added to my training the careers of coaching and mentoring. In 2005, I completed the Co-Active Life Coaching program from CTI (Coaching Training Institute), one of the foremost establishments on this topic.

This training program which consists of 5 weeks spread out over the period of a year provides a total of 16 hours of training. After this, I worked as a volunteer doing coaching in London.

Later I for an advanced degree of training on this topic, between 2008 and 2009 at the London-based Academy of Executive Coaching, I completed the diploma program for Advanced Executive Coaching. At the end of this advanced degree program, I completed the international certification and am still working in this field as a Certified International Executive Coach. Included in this, I am contributing to the development of this profession by serving as the chair of the board of the directors for EMCC Turkey which is included in the European Mentorship and Coaching Council*. At the same time under the structure of the Institute of Executive Coaching & Mentoring**, I am supporting the formation of the coaching training. At the same time, I am a member of ICF Turkey (International Coaching Federation)***.

---

*   http://www.emccouncil.org
** www.ioecm.com
*** http://www.coachfederation.org

In recent years, I am working on the concept of **corporate well-being** adding meaning to the implementation of coaching and mentoring.

I also as a part-time visiting professor at universities share with the university young people the information I have stored up on topics such as finance, brand management, and international relations. Until today I have been teaching classes as Izmir Economic University and Kadir Has University along with teaching for 3 years at Bosphorus University.

Conferences and Seminars:

In addition to these, I am a speaker and sitting chairman at international conferences on topics such as energy, structured trade, and investment financing as well as the transition to a low-carbon economy. You can follow and find information about all of my activities in the corresponding section on my website as well as my future activities at Twitter/rizakadilar .

Social Responsibility and My Experiences with Social Society Establishments:

As an active world citizen, I made it my mission to take an active role in civil society establishments that I believe will contribute toward providing positive change in the society in which we live.

In connection to this, if we set aside the Turkish Student Association of France (Les Etudiants Turcs en France) that we established in 1994 (known by very few people), my first real experience in this field for me was bringing to life the JCI (Junior Chamber International (www.jci.cc).

Like many famous leaders have said, I also in one sense learned "life" in this fellowship (especially about humans and my first experiences with politics and management).

Every year every duty changed at this association. I had various duties both in Turkey and in Holland where I lived for a time (which is why I am a lifetime honorary member in the JCI Amstelland) as well as in the international management. But probably the most important in the field were when I was a trainer at the 2002 Istanbul European Conference and, after being a participant in 1997, my 10-years as a trainer for the JCI European Leadership Academy.

I directed the 40th European Conference that happened in Istanbul in 2002. After exactly 6 years of working selflessly, the emergence of this conference has one of the most special places in my past life experiences.

Thanks to this conference being held outside the European Union for the first time, JCI Turkey made very important gains, and it became a great opportunity to promote our country. In the JCI organization that the 2002 Istanbul conference is still known as one of the most successful conferences thus far remains a source of pride for myself and for all my friends who labored. In the JCI structure I have duties as an instructor (for example, as the designer of and a trainer in the Leadership Academy of Turkey, as a guest speaker in the COC Academy in Austria and the designer of and trainer at the TOYP Academy) and as Senator number 59038 my ties to this fellowship are continuing forever...

Starting with JCI you will see that my experience with civil society establishments has continued and has developed a lot in recent years.

In our day, I am a member of many associations and have an active role in the revival of or the establishment of many associations. Of those, I'd like to touch on a few that are especially exciting:

I am a member of the scientific committee "Institut de Bosphore"* which was brought to life in the TÜSİAD organization. Like many valuable names who are world leaders on these topics, the reason for my taking a role in this institution is because of the sorrow that I've felt due the negative communication that began in the 2000s between the French and the Turkish people who had, for the length of history, a closeness, a solidarity, and a reciprocal cultural influence. The separation from this historical demarcation will affect even future generations. As one who is a leader on these topics, like many valuable names, the reason I have a role in this institution is that for their whole history as one who has had a great closeness, cooperation, and cultural interaction, I feel great sadness that the French and Turkish populations of the 2000s have separated from these historical lines and they are entering

---

* http://www.institut-bosphore.org

into negative communication that will affect even future generations. I believe that through the Institut de Bosphore and other many similar ventures the positive historical heritage between these 2 nations needs to be conveyed to future generations.

I am the founding president of ESU Turkey (English Speaking Union, www.esu.org). In the world in "general dialog" has to be established between individuals. It's an institution that was first established in 1914 in London and in our day, is continuing work in 50 countries providing for the development of reciprocal understanding among societies with the aim of contributing to world peace. Among our main activities are efforts such as public speaking competitions, English conversation gatherings and student and educator exchange programs. Since the association was established at the start of 2010, ESU Turkey, an association I believe in, is smaller although I hope it's activities in line with its goals, in one way or another, will greatly contribute to the development of a culture of tolerant dialog in our country.

Hisar Education Association (HEV):

Our acquaintance starting as a parent of a child in the Hisar schools, as of June 2012 is continuing as a member of the board of trustees for the Hisar Education Association (HEV). This place where our daughter studied, this precious educational establishment will constitute an example for the educational system in our country. It's a place to which I'm excited to contribute to it being a special establishment which will train and to which we will be able to entrust our youth who are our future.*

CFoT:

I took on the coordination of CFoT. (Conservative Friends of Turkey, UK www.cfot.org.uk, was established in the organization of the British Conservative Party) You will find detailed information about this formation on the related website. This formation was actually made to be a channel for communication. In this respect, the formation sees its duty as a bridge between both the Turkish population living in England with

---

* www.hisarschool.k12.tr

the Conservative Party and also Turkey with the Conservative Party. I believe that especially in the period ahead of us it will serve a role as a communication channel making positive contributions to the process of Turkey becoming a member of the European Union.

GYİAD:

It is my old flame... While the dear Şerif Kaynar was the chair, as a part of a project to reverse brain migration, I became a member of this association of which these days I am a member of the board of directors. In the last period, as the chair of the Commission for Member and Social Society Establishment Relations, we signed on to a series of activities with the goal of creating added-value, positive dialog within the membership network of GYIAD as well as with members of similar associations. As for this period as co-chairs of the Commission for Social Society Establishments and Public Relations, we are working in these fields to contribute to the development of our members who are in these fields. You can follow these efforts at Twitter/rizakadilar.

TÜGİAD:

This is one of the most precious associations for young businessmen in our country. I am also the chair of the ISEGE (Work and Strategic Development).

DEİK:

In this valuable establishment of ours, I am the Vice President of the Turkish-Korean Work Council and serve on the executive board of directors of the Turkish-Indian and Turkish-Belgium work councils. There is a separate, different professional reason all to its own for my having a place on these countries' executive boards...

The Co-Chair of the HEC Turkey Graduates Association:

This group that I was chair of with my dear friend Ari Meşulam, comes into prominence as one of the world's most outstanding schools in our country as a representing body. Paris-based "HEC" is actually, in general, a well-known school in the world. For years its MBA program has been selected as the best MBA. At the same time throughout the world, HEC is 6th for having the most graduates who are CEOs the Fortune 500 companies. As for in our country, is a small but very decent group of graduates. In the period ahead of us, we are going to work to make the school more known in our country, and we are going to introduce graduates from similar schools to HEC graduates.

eXeC Turkey:

As the 3rd sector, eXec Turkey* is one of my latest efforts in the transitive world of civil society organizations. With the goal of providing coaching services to upper-level managers and providing the needed support to those who make the decisions concerning the improvement of the implementation of corporate governance, I established the Istanbul-based think tank, Executive Management Excellence Center (eXeC Turkey). You can follow our efforts in this field at Twitter/execturkey.

Energy and Climate Change Foundation:

In our day, especially the carbon cycle has come to the forefront as an international political component. Falling on me as an individual to mindfully support the formation of the Energy and Climate Change Foundation in which after its establishment I desired to take an active role, this foundation promotes the carrying out of needed scientific work on this important topic in our country in one way to be a carbon efficient economy and for us in this context to leave to the next generations a more livable world.

You can follow my ideas and my efforts on this topic of carbon efficiency with this independent foundation at Twitter/lowcarbonturkey. Of course, my desire is that you will look glance at my blog that you will find at lowcarbonturkey.com as well as my Facebook page on this topic.

My work on the topic of corporate governance:

In the years I was in London, with the title of "company secretary" taking a role on the board of directors under the supervision of the Finan-

---

* www.execturkey.com

cial Services Authority (FSA), I actively worked on the topic of "Corporate Governance" and prepared training. In this field, I am a member of IoD (Institute of Director www.iod.co.uk) and the TKYD (Turkish Corporate Management Foundation www.tkyd.org/tr). My articles on this topic are found in different magazines (cf. the "in the press" corner of my website). Since I believe that corporate governance of family companies is possible along with majority shareholding initiatives and ownership, I believe that providing support with "executive coaching" during the phase of a company's becoming corporate is needed.

One of the new things I'm excited about in recent days is independent membership on a board. I found the first opportunity in this area with AFM Cinemas. Along with Esas Holding, one of our country's foremost private equity groups, Actera's majority shareholder is Mars Entertainment Group of which Actera is a subsidiary. In the May 2012 I was chosen by Actera's general board according to SPK rules as a non-executive independent board member. At the same time, I also took on the duty as the chair of the supervisory committee. I hope that this will be a great opportunity for me to bring to life what I have stored up in this field up until now.

ÇİTAM:

"And of course, the world is changing. Under the name of an "axis shift", the position the West had gained in the last few centuries is slowly sliding to the East. To monitor this process of change more closely, there will be an information bridge between one of the world's new leaders, China, and our country, and for the businessmen of these two countries and thought leaders, we have designed a think tank which will come into prominence as a source of information, the Chinese-Turkish Research Center* which signed into its first activities in June 2012. In the formation stage, I am very pleased to be the father of this idea and to lead this organization."

Is there anything else that I need to explain, read or mention? Actually, this Curriculum Vitae in some respects may be changed from 2013 until today. However, probably he added

---

*   www.chinainstituteturkey.com

more duties and he wrote down 2 more books which it's one of them its leaderships book: **From Competence to Leader** and the other name is: **China.**

– **It's really amazing...I'd like to return again to other "real professionals". In addition to Muhtar Kent, Dr. Oz and Dr. Kadilar, who are some others you think we could mention?**
– There definitely are. But basically, what stands out most...

It's always important to receive inspiration from important people by reading their biographies. Years ago, one of our first-year economics teachers in university, Professor Kamil Yılmaz made a statement I still haven't forgotten. I don't know what the topic of biographies was opened in class, but he said, *"I'm always reading biographies. I've benefited from them greatly. You read, and you will benefit greatly."*

Since I was already a person who was interested in these types of topics, these words motivated me. However, whose and which people's biographies you read are important. On top of that, most of the people I'm going to mention don't have biographies. This is also one of our shortcomings. The writing of biographies is actually very important. Because we have much to learn from the lives of role models. **There, the experience was gained and is waiting and ready. Why should we go through this experience again? Smart societies are ones that benefit from the experience.**

Furthermore, no matter what, we will live through our experiences again. Our own experiences are a plus for us. That's how it must be. However, especially need to benefit from "real professionals'" experiences. You want a name from me. Only, I'd like to say this. I'm going to explain to you only as much as I can from their resumes. When it comes a time, I will mention their relevance to our principles. I'd like our friends who are reading this talk to research these names. That is better.

When do you think you learn the best?

– **When researching?**
– Being curious and researching... Yes, these are true.

However, you learn the best when you are forced to teach a discourse on a topic.

When you feel like a teacher.

This is critical. If it were up to me, I'd have students "teach" and "lead" some classes. Students need to become an expert in a topic and communicate it to the others. Actually, this whole educational system needs to spread.

Do you know who Professor Onur Güntürkün is? The Turkish Hawking?

– I hear about him from you...

– Then I suppose what I will explain to you now will be enough.

Kemal Yalçın wrote a fabulous book called **"Vitality"**.* It is the life story of distinguished Professor Onur Güntürkün. Onur Güntürkün is a perfect academician and of course a real professional indeed...

Onur Güntürkün will receive a Nobel Prize one day. Kemal Yalçın has a great set of works. Furthermore, I suggest visiting Mr. Kemal's website and receiving more information at kemalyalcin.com. Mr. Yalçın is a very special person. From poems and biographies of bilingual children's books, he is someone who has many products in many different areas.

So, I do share with you the summary of the life of Onur Güntürkün with Mr. Yalçın words:

A Story of Pride...

A Star in the Universe of the Brain: Distinguished Professor Onur Güntürkün

Research of the brain is one of the most quickly developing scientific branches in our day. According to estimates, what is known about the brain multiplies by 2-fold every 8 years. Despite this, science still can only shed light on a small portion of the universe of the brain. Every new discovery and information that is arrived at is the start of a new investigation.

---

* http://www.idefix.com/Kitap/Yasama-Gucu/Kemal-Yalcin/Edebiyat/Turk-Gunluk-Ani/urunno=0000000445065

Thousands of scientists are working to expand the borders of our information about the universe of the brain and are trying to illuminate the unknown.

Distinguished Professor Onur Güntürkün is one of the foremost scientists in the world with his discoveries, investigations and scientific articles that he has written on the brain.

Onur Güntürkün took his place in the scientific world by overcoming significant difficulties, by swimming in the sea that he created himself and by turning hopelessness into hope.

His education, discoveries, and awards:

The road that brought Onur Güntürkün to today, is science's formidable but honorable path.

He was born in Izmir (Turkey) in 1958. He finished primary school in 1969 in Baden-Baden, Germany. He was forced to quit the Richard Wagner New Languages High School in this city in the middle of 8th grade. He continued his high school education beginning the second half of 1973 at the Izmir Atatürk High School. He received his high school diploma from this school.

For his university education, he returned to Germany. He registered in September 1975 in the Psychology Department at Bochum University. In the third semester, he became a student class called "The Implementation of Experimental Psychology" taught by Argentine professor Juan Delius.

He chose the topic of reorganization in the brain for his diploma thesis. For his diploma thesis research, he began research on a pigeon brain in 1978 with Juan Delius at his side. At that time, it was thought that the brain of a pigeon was similar to that of a human. While working on his diploma work, on the other hand, he also participated in the seminars that Delius taught on electrophysiological mechanisms in the brain and methods for measuring electric currents in the brain.

He was honored for his very successful thesis work with a rating of "very good". He was given the job status of an assistant researcher at Bochum University.

On September 1, 1980, with the salary of a part-time assistant, he began his doctorate thesis at Professor Juan Delius's side. At that time, what got Onur Güntürkün's attention was the difference in functions of the right and left sides of the human brain. The scientific name of this matter was "Lateralization". He chose this for this doctoral thesis. Despite the topic of "lateralization" being important from a clinical perspective, in the 1980s there wasn't much information on this topic.

Onur Güntürkün began a long and tiring research on this little-known field. With the experiments that he conducted, he proved to the world for the first time that lateralization also took place in pigeons. This became his first discovery in the scientific world. Up until that time, it was believed by the whole world that right and left half spheres of the pigeon brain were the same. Experiments were designed according to this view. Onur Güntürkün with his scientific experiments destroyed this view at its foundation. This breakthrough was a seminal and very important step in the fields of electrophysiology and lateralization. In 1983 due to this discovery, the "Bochum University Superior Research Award" was given to Onur Güntürkün.

This award was his first.

Onur Güntürkün completed his doctoral work in 1984 with the of the distinction of "Stellar Excellent" or the Latin Summa Cum Laude.

In 1987 earning the German Research Fund Scholarship, he went to America. He advanced the research in the Professor Harvey Karten's laboratory, a very important, world-renown brain scientist working at San Diego University.

In January 1988, he returned from America and began working in the assistant cadre to Professor Juan Delius's professorial chair at Konstanz University.

In 1992, he finishes his Habilitation work. His docent thesis was accepted.

In 1993, he was honored with the "Gerhard Hess Science Award" by the German Research Fund.

On April 1, 1993, along with the summer semester, he was appointed the professorial chair under which he had done his doctoral work and had worked as an assistant, in place of his professor, Juan Delius.

1995 Krupp Science Award

Onur Güntürkün in 1980 began brain research using pigeons as a model. In 1983, he began the work on Lateralization, that is the research on reasons as to the difference between the right and left sides of the brain; the structure of the brain; connections in the brain and systems in the brain. The research and scientific discoveries that began in 1980 were rewarded in 1995 with the "Krupp Science Award", one of Germany's most prestigious awards.

At the award ceremony Dr. Johannes Rau, who in those years was the prime minister of the North Ren Vestfalya State, gave a meaningful speech. He expressed these things about Onur Güntürkün:

"I want to underscore a few points about the scientist to whom this award is being given. Onur Güntürkün has two homelands. He didn't live in Izmir only at the moment of his birth. He spent his childhood there and finished high school over there. As for primary and middle school, they were completed in Germany.

Onur Güntürkün...his two homelands... the heart of Germany and Turkey. I find it very delightful that the award is being given to a scientist who has the heart of two homelands.

Onur Güntürkün is not once said, 'At one time I was Turkish, but now I am German.'

Onur Güntürkün never said 'I'm Turkish. I'm just a visitor here.'

Dear Professor Onur Güntürkün is living in two languages, in two cultures, in two countries' scientific worlds, and in two countries' traditions.

I especially want to touch on this.

Onur Güntürkün is a person who never forgot he was a Turk. I am particularly pleased with this. This is why I am celebrating him from the heart. I feel great pride in giving this type of scientist this great award."

Rau gave the 1995 Krupp Science Award to Güntürkün after his speech.

During the conversation time, he came to Güntürkün. Freely, emotionally he gave a brief and genuine speech. He explained in his opinion the importance of this work and what his work was about. Explaining why he was in love with science and why being in science was the best work in the world, he finished his words in this way:

"Do you know that all that I've done, continually desiring to help people, I'm doing to cure diseases?

The results of my research and my scientific findings make the lives of people richer. They can be used for the benefit of people and treatment of patients. If these become reality, I will greatly rejoice.

But if I say, "I am doing this for science." It's a lie. Because my main desire is to know. I do my work and my research because I have been caught in an eternal passion for science.

Since I have succumbed to the craving to find something new, every morning I go running to the university, to my lab. It's as if you're like Christopher Columbus wandering around in the ocean in a sailboat for life. You yourself are Christopher Columbus to little islands. That huge continent was discovered. Even if it isn't a continent, you are discovering the tiny islands in the ocean.

This is the essence of science. Without this passion, this excitement, science is impossible."

Onur Güntürkün, with this understanding, with this passion, continued his efforts. In 1997, he rose to the highest scientific rank of **Distinguished Professor**.

Relations with Turkey:

Along with his scientific work, he also made time for his social efforts. Bochum University and Istanbul University became sister universities through his efforts. At present, the burden of the relationship between these two universities falls on his shoulders.

Onur Güntürkün has a place not only in the German scientific world but at the same time in the Turkish scientific world.

In 1996, he went to Izmir for a period of 6 months. He worked to contribute to the scientific research on the matter of brain research at Ege and Dokuz Eylül Universities. He gave lectures at Muğla and Boğaziçi Universities.

He went to a mountain in Kuşköy (bird village) in order to conduct research and experiments regarding a whistled language, which is spoken in only three places in the world and in Turkey only in Kuşköy in the Black Sea region. With the equipment for the experiments that he set up in the coffeehouse, he conducted scientific investigations with the people who speak the whistled language. He researched the brain functions of these people.

In 2000 Onur Güntürkün was given the title "Honorary Doctor" by Istanbul University. In 2006 because of his superior successes in national and international biopsychology field, he was awarded the "Wilhelm-Wundt Medal" by the German Psychological Society.

His over 170 articles worthy of high science, his publication and books were spoken of with respect. In 2007, he was also awarded the Special Science Award by the Scientific Research Council of Turkey (TÜBİTAK).

Onur Güntürkün Place in the Scientific World:

I asked about Onur Güntürkün's place in the scientific world and his recent discoveries. He answered this way:

"In recent months, we have reached some interesting results. According to one theory that has been put forward for a long time, the reason that the brain is asymmetrical is that it saves the two half-spheres of the brain from doing the same work. The other of each of the brain's hemispheres cut in two the neural capacity for performing separate tasks. The assumption of the theory is this, but up until now, no one has been able to show whether this was true or false.

Just now we have been able to obtain the first concrete results. We were able to show with the pigeons in my laboratory that they used while measuring the electric currents of with the pigeons in my laboratory, measuring only the electric currents of the visual system in the right and left hemispheres of the nucleus of the Thalamus region, we were able to show that these neurons use separate analysis mechanisms in the left and right hemispheres. In this research, we are approaching the side of one brain cell with .005mm wide electrodes and investigating its working mechanisms. We conduct this research with the pigeons doing various tasks and while making decisions among different selections.

In general, we've determined that the neurons in the left hemisphere analyze the basic components of the stimuli that the animal sees. On the other hand, we were able to show that the neurons in the right hemisphere rather stay under the effect of the higher brain centers. This means that the working mechanisms of these cells function not according to the details of the stimulus but according to the expectations of the animal. This left-right distinction complies with the 'bottom-up' (from heel to head) and 'top-down' (from head to heel) dilemma.

To be able to show this is a very important discovery. Because it shows that the animal model that we were using was accurate even though that hypothesis that had been debated for a long time. We want to publish this discovery of our soon.

I'm working on different topics. The research we are doing with the right and left distinctions of the brain are with both pigeons and with people. In recent years, I started doing research with dolphins. I have a doctoral student who is living in Mallorca and working on this topic. Furthermore, a large portion of my lab is researching the relative memory mechanisms of the prefrontal cortex.

It was not known whether or not there is symmetry in dolphin brains. These animals, 70 million years ago, are one of 3 groups of mammals that while living on land returned again to the water. The dolphins' current closest relatives living on the land are the hippopotamus and animals like cattle. The return from the land to the sea 60-70 million years ago is the reason for the important changes in their brains. Therefore, we are researching the changes in the dolphin brain and the effects on its asymmetry. We were able to show that they really are cerebral asymmetry in the dolphin brain. Even though the structures of the dolphin brain changed much from the brains of their land-dwelling relatives, the principle of the brain's asymmetric organization stayed the same. Most recently, I am working on the question of whether or not there is asymmetry in the dolphin's system of communication."

The status of the Relationship between Bochum University and Istanbul University:

To the questions, "What will the scientific results be of the fraternity between Bochum University and Istanbul University? On what types of scientific projects are you working?" Onur Güntürkün gave the following answer:

"Bochum University and Istanbul University are similar to each other in many ways. Both are very large universities. Both have potential and desire for scientific research in every department and in every discipline of study. Bochum University, just like Istanbul University want to shine in science.

As far as students are concerned, there are similarities between in those at each university. At Bochum University, there are close to 2,000 students of Turkish origin or those with Turkish citizenship. As for Istanbul University, there are many students who did their primary and middle school studies in Germany. These students know German well.

For Turkey and Germany, it is a good opportunity to have students studying in both universities who know Turkish and German well. At both universities, we established an exchange program. So far 30 students have come from Istanbul. Thirty students also went from Bochum University to Istanbul. Not all the students who have gone to Istanbul University are Turkish. German students are also going. These students are learning the language, receiving an education, bringing the experiences that they have obtained and are finding opportunities to learn more about the country to which they have gone.

Furthermore, the exchange scientists also happen between these two sister universities. They are working on common scientific projects. I'd like to see an increase in all of these relationships. But this is what we are able to do thus far with the current resources."

If it weren't for Turkey, Onur Güntürkün also wouldn't exist.

Without Germany, perhaps the scientific world would have been deprived of scientists like Onur Güntürkün. As Dr. Johannes Rau stated, he is the beating heart of the science fields in both Germany and Turkey.

He is a source of pride for both Germans and Turks. He is a prominent star lighting up the universe of the brain.

— **An unbelievable story. I'll definitely read this book...**
— Actually, there are more amazing parts. I'd like to express this here. Onur Güntürkün is overcoming another hardship. He had a brush with death. I'd like to briefly summarize this from Can Dündar's writing:

"*A Child Named Onur*

Our story begins on August 18, 1962, in Zonguldak.

On that day while returning from the beach, 4-year-old Onur fell from his bicycle. His right foot was cut on a rusty boat. During the night, he became feverish. When he awoke, he was like jelly. He became paralyzed.

He could see, understand and speak but couldn't move.

After 9 months of treatment in Turkey, they brought him to his uncle living in Germany.

The doctors gave the condition that he must learn German in order for the treatment to be successful. Saying to his mother, "He absolutely mustn't speak Turkish" they accepted him.

Staying all by himself in a wheelchair, for weeks he cried alone.

At the end of 8 months after learning German, his family settled in Germany.

Using corsets and braces he began walking drills.

After a long period of treatment, he was able to move his hands and arms but not be able to walk.

In his school, he was the only handicapped person and only Turk.

He was studying and undergoing difficult spinal cord surgeries.

For a present, for his birthday he requested a microscope. His peculiarities began to appear.

While the children were in religion and physical education classes, he was alone in the lawn he was mapping the ants' domain, and he drew on paper the shapes of the feet of the bugs he had collected and was inspecting.

Most of his time was spent in the library.

Giving himself completely to reading, he passed his peers.

Do Fish See Colors?

After finishing middle school, they returned to Turkey, their permission for residency having finished.

Onur began school in 1973 at Izmir Atatürk High School. He transferred with appreciation. His aim was to study psychology. While in his 3rd year of high school in TÜBİTAK's science experiment competition, he made finals with his experiment proving that fish see the world as black and white. He didn't receive a prize, but in him, a fire was started to unlock the mysteries of nature.

Finishing high school at the top of his class, he returned to Germany for the university."

– I was too quick to conclude it was unbelievable...
– I told you. There's no need for much commentary. From what I read above, the resume, autobiography and the excerpt notice three basic characteristics:

1. How did Onur Güntürkün use his **time**?
2. What stages did he pass through to develop and achieve **expertise**, and what difficulties did he endure?
3. How did he develop **relationships management and social intelligence**? How did he establish national and international relationships? What were his goals in heading this direction?

– I'm guessing it's time for the 5th professional...
– Precisely. Actually, we could make this list pretty long. There are many valuable managers, academicians, reporters, and doctors.

One of the real professionals that have gotten my attention is **Ali Nasuh Mahruki**, an out and out sportsman and civil society leader. He is a **Snow Leopard**. What I know is that Nasuh Mahruki graduated in 1992 from Bilkent University. However, again, as far as I know, the date that he started professional mountaineering is 1991.

That is, he became a professional before graduating. I think that his experiences in university were important. Bilkent University raised quite significant graduates. However, Nasuh Mahruki is proof of what roads can be opened up in the environment of a **"free university"**. Since there he discovers mountaineering at the Natural Sports Club activities, and I'm assuming at that time the seeds of curiosity were sown. The year is 1988.

– **How does one become a Snow Leopard?**
– The title of Snow Leopard is given to those who climb 5 mountains that are higher than 7000 meters and within the borders of the ex-Soviet Union. The numbers of these people aren't too many. If I need to explain, he was the first Turk to climb Mount Everest and the first Muslim mountain climber.

In 1996, he became the 45th sportsman and the youngest to complete the **Seven Summits** project by climbing the highest mountains on the 7 continents. In later years, he accomplished many tough climbs. The most important ones were those he did without oxygen, mountains Cho Oyu, Lhotse, and K2.

After 15 years, he climbed Mount Everest again. We know that he organized many speeches and seminars on topics such as leadership, teamwork, personal development, self-knowledge, goal-orientation, decisiveness, discipline and risk management.

If you want to learn what leadership and motivation are, you need to listen to Nasuh Mahruki. As far as I know, he wrote 7 books. I especially recommend the last 2:

The one he wrote in 2007, **"The Homeland is Loved with Actions Not Words"** and the one everyone must read whose aim is to be conscientious, **"Climb Your Own Everest"** which he wrote in 2010.

Ali Nasuh Mahruki for many reasons is a real professional. No one can say anything against his time management and expertise. It's impossible. But I think his most important characteristics are his relationship management and social intelligence.

I see in him the **"Michael Jordan spirit"**.

– **Exactly what is this "Michael Jordan spirit?"**

– The "Michael Jordan spirit" is this: very courteous, noble.

There's an expression that the Americans have that I really like: "To challenge", "To fly in the face of", to have a defiant spirit. He challenges you in a kind way. Opposite that person, you are crushed in 2 ways. He is powerful, very skillful and very polite.

I call this the politeness tactic. He crushes you with it. At least let's say that's how he was in front of the public. This spirit is very important. The search and rescue association "AKUT"* might have been established solely with the "Michael Jordan spirit". Under normal conditions, the establishment of AKUT is nearly impossible in this country.

I know this quite well since I have worked for years in civil society establishments, and am still leading 2 groups.

I can surmise quite well most particularly how many difficulties had to be tolerated in order to establish an association that conducts search and rescue operations, to keep it afloat and to keep operations going. However, if you were to ask me about Ali Nasuh Mahruki's leadership and go-getter characteristics, my interpretation is that it is a genetical inheritance along with a "Michael Jordan spirit". Moreover, he summarized himself in his book

"The Homeland is Loved with Actions Not Words" on pages 31-34:

The son of Mr. Mehmet Ali, that is the father my grandfather Eşref Cafer Bey, after finishing at Galatasaray High School** and Mülkiye***, studied at Sorbonne University, learned 6 languages, taught at Mülkiye, served in embassy jobs in various Caucasus countries and in India and delivered significant help from the Indian Muslims to Turkey during the years of the Balkan War.

The son of Mr. Eşref Cafer, that is my grandfather, Ali Cevat Mahruki, studied in Hungary, and as a young construction engineer of the new Turkish Republic signed off on a great number of projects. As one of the founders of Garanti Bank was a member of the board of directors from its establishment until 1952.

---

*   akut.org.tr/en
** gsl.gsu.edu.tr/en/
*** politics.ankara.edu.tr/english/

Ali Cevat Mahruki's son, that is my father Cafer Cem Mahruki, was one of Turkey's best collectors of money and was the president of the "Turkish Numismatics Association".

As for Ali Nasuh Mahruki, the son of Cem Mahruki, trying his whole life to be worthy of the family whose blood he carries and is a member of, is a driver but unfortunately thinks that he has been wronged can be described with an old expression, "he's a one-of-a-kind" man.

Actually, the whole story is this basic..."

Yes, actually his story is this basic...

– **There are many topics to talk about. I know well since in your seminars you touch on many different topics. However, I want to bring our conversation to an end here. In the last year, we met at different times and made this conversation happen. Are there any final words you would like to add?**

– Above all, I'd like to thank you. For a period of over one year, you have listened to me without becoming bored. At times, we were forced to take a break.

After these conversations, we will talk about regarding 2 basic national issues with you which are not too much interesting for international readers, that's why we will add those conversations after our main conversation. In book format, there will be added as additional sections...

For my final words, I'd like to say this. Let's not ever forget the 5-wings windmill.

Work life is not all there is in life! Life is very rich.

You can do many things in life. Maybe some things not right away, but extending over a period of time, facing it with **persistence,** in the end, you will do it.

When a person is strong intellectually, artistically, sportswise and socially, he can enjoy his work. Otherwise, work life is a heavy burden and makes it easy for you to become a truly depressive case.

As a final word, I'm saying;

"Never Look Back! You Are Not Going That Way!"...

Love to all...

EPILOGUE

When I first went into the business scene, there were a lot of unhappy people around me. Presently, they still are. Before now, I had been thinking that only people who couldn't achieve their career objectives were unhappy. But with the passage of time, I realized that even people who managed to realize their set goals could even be unhappy. On the other hand, I have met a lot of people who were able to remain happy despite their low paying jobs or careers.

So, where does this contradiction takes its source from? Even though they are successful and envied by all, why are these people so unhappy? How can one be unsuccessful in business and yet be happy?

When I have personal conversations with "Successful" but unhappy people, I usually get these answers:

"I planned very clear goals. I succeeded in achieving all, but I couldn't keep a family relationship together. I eventually got divorced. My daughter is not even talking to me. I miss the old days."

"I'm at the summit point of my career. However, when it comes to the things that I do, I don't enjoy it. I have always worked for the next level. Now, when I look back to those times, I ask myself, "Was it worth it?"

"I loved my job. Then unavoidably, politics entered into my business. I actually did what I had to. Now, I really don't know whom to trust."

These are very serious and hard problems which may destroy someone's life.

I classify unhappy people into two categories. Nevertheless, both categories end up the same way. There is only a time difference between them.

First ones are the people whose careers and goals are determined by others. For this group, the meaning of "success" has been determined by their family, friends, environment, and society. You have to be a CEO, you have to rise through directorship. These people struggle to become what they are told to be and achieve set goals from high school years. The interesting part is they are not aware how fast time passes while they are struggling with all of these. They think they will be happy when they achieve those goals, and see that as a price in return for hard work. For this group, most of them discover that they have been on the wrong track after they reach the summit of their carriers.

The second group happens to be the ones who start their lives with nice dreams, but in the long run, they are losing their focus because of pressure they face from their family or the environment. For example, I know people who have become doctors to heal people with real desire. Most of them are changed by money, and the desire is put away as their second plan. They have a lot now, but they are not happy. They struggle with the void that occurred by the lost meaning of life. And it is not very possible for them to fill this void. If you see a doctor who wanders joyless along the corridors of hospitals, he/she may be emotionally weak, longing for happiness and incredibly fragile.

There is only one way to be really happy, **"creating values"**. You can create the value as a CEO, or as a worker of a company. Your level of happiness will increase or decrease, depending on the value that you will create. For this, it is very important for you to apply the principles presented in this book. However, it does not end with choosing your career because there are too many value-creating ways in a single job. An engineer, for example, can build historical buildings, create some magnificent designs and make his/her customers happy or he can make more people happy by helping them own their own homes by building low-priced structures.

It's up to you alone to define which one is going to make you happy, so don't let others influence you, because the advice given, are usually the projections of worries and weaknesses of the ones who give them. These people who actually wish good for you may unconsciously force you to a lifetime of unhappiness.

For this, make a self-evaluation when you are on the edge to choose your job. Answer these questions, "What do I expect from business life except earning money and making a career?", "What do I enjoy doing?", "How can I contribute?", "What will I leave behind when I retire?". The answers you'll give to these questions will help you to clear your **"Life purpose"**.

For all the things, you will do, later on, take this purpose as your reference. Compare different alternatives for their basic benefits to your life.

With this, you can be sure that your career is on the right path.

Your life purpose will also raise your inner consistency, and strengthen your self-integrity. This kind of strong reference will block you from wrong ways that may last very heavily for you, by falling in life's stream. Never forget that no one says, "I wish I earned more money, dressed cooler or changed the car's model" when they are on their deathbed. When you come to the last point, created values and impact made are most important.

Fare well to you and good luck.
Professor Türker Baş
Founder of New HR Consulting Group

"I am not leaving behind a verse, a dogma or a hard-set, rigid rule as a spiritual heritage.
My spiritual heritage is SCIENCE and MIND. Those who come after me will appreciate the tough and deep-seated difficulties that we faced and were forced to overcome. Perhaps we didn't fully reach our goals, but they will endorse our never swerving from having MIND and SCIENCE as our guide.
Time is quickly advancing; the perceptions nations, societies and people have even of happiness and unhappiness are changing.
To assert that this sort of world was brought about by rules that will never change is to deny the development of MIND and SCIENCE.
What I wanted to do for the Turkish Nation, and what I worked to achieve are apparent. After me, if those who desire to embrace me accept as their guide the foundational axis of MIND and SCIENCE, then they are my spiritual heirs."

Mustafa Kemal Atatürk*

---

* According to Professor Arnold M. Ludwig, the first leader of the 20th century is Mustafa Kemal Atatürk. Mr. Ludwig developed a serious methodology when choosing the world leaders. "King of the Mountain" presents the startling findings of Arnold M. Ludwig's eighteen-year investigation into why people want to rule. The answer may seem obvious -- power, privilege, and perks -- but any adequate answer also needs to explain why so many rulers

Additional Sections:
1. EMPLOYMENT IN TURKEY, UNEMPLOYMENT, AND THE INFORMAL ECONOMY

– At this point, I'd like to ask you some more open questions concerning unemployment and career life. How much unemployment is there in this country?
– There is an institution in Ankara called the Turkish Statistical Institute. Its abbreviation is TSI.

---

cling to power even when they are miserable, trust nobody, feel besieged, and face almost certain death. Ludwig's results suggest that leaders of nations tend to act remarkably like monkeys and apes in the way they come to power, govern, and rule. Profiling every ruler of a recognized country in the twentieth century -- over 1,900 people in all Ludwig establishes how rulers came to power, how they lost power, the dangers they faced, and the odds of their being assassinated, committing suicide, or dying a natural death. Then, concentrating on a smaller sub-set of 377 rulers for whom more extensive personal information was available, he compares six different kinds of leaders, examining their characteristics, their childhoods, and their mental stability or instability to identify the main predictors of later political success. Ludwig's penetrating observations, though presented in a lighthearted and entertaining way, offer important insight into why humans have engaged in war throughout recorded history as well as suggesting how they might live together in peace.

To buy the book: amazon.com/gp/product/B00CEAAY8M/ref=oh_au-i_d_detailpage_o00_?ie=UTF8&psc=1

It's an institution for which I have a lot of respect. Nevertheless, this is how the situation: It is not wise to completely trust the data put out by a government or their corroborating firms, not just with this government but anyone who is in power. No one takes offense, but this is the truth.

Do you remember that at one time in Turkey there was a debate about ombudsmanship?

– **Yes, how could I not know? And, as you know, the first step was taken: the parliament elected the first ombudsman...**
– The ombudsman is my most loved and in developed countries an indispensable institution. There is an ombudsman in Turkey. In fact, he has his own organization. Do you know the name of this person? Do you remember? No one knows!

This is because we made the decision very quickly and without debating in front of the public. We did this work only to have done it. We did it with the election methods of bringing a law into existence. I'm not thinking it was debated for too long in the committees, at least it didn't grab my attention.

Let's learn what this institution is about:

Looking at the root of the word, in Swedish *ombuds* with the meaning "mediator" and *man* meaning "person" make up the word "ombudsman", resulting in the definition "mediator person". You will understand that his person must be a unique human being. He must carry a lot of weight.

The word *ombudsman* in Swedish usually is used to refer to a delegate, a lawyer, a representative or another person who is given the authority to act on the part of an individual or a group of people in order to protect their rights.

Corporately, the term *ombudsman* denotes someone or a group of people who are chosen by parliament to listen to the people's grievances and to arrive at solutions. Turkish equivalents to *ombudsman* such as a public controller, mediator, public arbitrator, defender of civil rights, Parliament commissioner were proposed.

To sum up, I want to say, the *ombudsman* is an independent public authority who is given the responsibility to find solutions to issues concerning the implementation of public services, record grievances by who are affected by them and conduct investigations.

So, I'd like to repeat: **ombudsman is an independent public authority**. Due to this, now we have an *ombudsman, TSI,* who can say that it is found that the unemployment numbers don't exactly reflect reality and that they aren't according to world standards.

When we complain about the topic will the ombudsman push TSI for the actual unemployment numbers? Will they be our representative?

– **It should be tried!**
– These types of systems create a very difficult situation for us. No matter what the economic system or institution, above everything, the statistics must accurately reflect reality. Or to state it more openly, to never be open to manipulation and for statistics to not be overly positive or negative but absolutely transparent in order to most benefit the country and the people.

If I had the authority, I would declare TSI a completely independent statistics and inventory institution, and I would even change its location.

In the same way that there is a project to bring the Central Bank to Istanbul, many organizations need to leave Ankara. The other independent organizations need to be distributed to our other cities. For example, BRSA (Banking Regulation and Supervision Agency) could go to Antalya. Why couldn't RTSC (Radio and Television Supreme Council) move to one of our Black Sea cities? In the same way, TSI must be completely independent. In fact, it needs to relocate to an eastern province, to Malatya for example. As far away from the political systems that these types of institutions can be, the better.

At this juncture, let there be no misunderstanding, I'm not suggesting a decentralization or a system of management.

I'm suggesting that the moving of the independent institutions to the four corners of the country would increase the level of concentration and motivation regarding their work and that the political effects could be reduced. Of course, it doesn't work to merely change the province. Even if there weren't independent institutions, unemployment rates would still rise and fall. Sometimes apples and pears are placed on top of one another. And then sometimes we say, "Oh, what's the need?" This time they are separated.

In the 2010s, the headline that unemployment figures fell between 8 and 9.6 percent came and went (the last number is 12,6 percent as for Feb. 2017) For a long while the TSI figures were right around these ratios.* But I am finding that these numbers actually need to be multiplied by four.

– So, you are saying in the 30-percentile range. Don't you think this number high?
– On the contrary, this number is optimistic even. Unemployment figures are actually deceiving. Because we are talking about a system that, in general, has wrong figures and faulty reference points. At this point, 30 percent might not even be reflecting the truth.

Particularly since in Turkey, a large portion of women workers is working off the books.

So, we aren't only incorrectly counting the unemployed, the employment numbers are also not correct.

So, you might wonder how a country that has so many workers "off the book" can have unemployment figures of between 8 and 9 percent? This is impossible. As one who has given speeches in the four corners of Turkey, I'm obligated to speak the truth. At least I'm trying to approach the truth. In Turkey today, neither the employment rates nor the unemployment rates are accurate.

– So, considering what you are saying if we were to figure the employment percentages according to the national population, there are 5 million unemployed workers.

---

* For the last numbers: http://www.tuik.gov.tr/HbGetirHTML.do?id=24941

– So that's what I'm saying. In Turkey how is the number for the part of the population labeled "working" is calculated? I also don't know this.

Are the "off the books" workers included in this number? It's being said that the estimate is between 38 and 41 percent (for last numbers please look at the deep note). As it is, if the employed population is 26 million, about half of these could be shown to be illegal.

I don't exactly understand how TSI is able to arrive at this explicit of a number of unregistered workers. *Precisely because they are unregistered, this number cannot be calculated.* Furthermore, how are you going to know what portion of the population is not working? I'm supposing that they gather together agricultural figures, some sectoral statistics, student numbers, retired persons and other statistics, guessing on some figures, they bring the statistics to a certain place. But this also doesn't satisfy me. I guess I need to do a one or two-week apprenticeship at TSI.

– **So, the youth unemployment figures?**
– For a long time, even TSI had the numbers for unemployed youth in the city at between 17 and 20 percent. (Feb 2017 number its 23 percent). According to this calculation, **the one in five youth living in the cities is without work.** I am of the opinion that this number is incorrectly reflected.

Of course, I don't have a company poll in my hand, and I don't own a huge website. I go everywhere and wander around. Young people send me emails, and I am in active contact with them. Believe me, this is a conservative figure.

Today, young people who have graduated from university have a low probability of finding work to their liking and in their profession. You might be able to say that this is known.

This problem from all along has now been revealed. Youth have become the most hopeless sector. We must be realists. We must coordinate the education, industry and the service sector as a whole.

– **I was going to ask what we should do, but you were faster...**

– I also want to ask you a question. In research that was done including 186 countries concerning women's representation in the workforce, in what place do you think Turkey is?
– **I can only say it's not in the first 50.**
– There is a journal titled "Kule" that Koç University publishes seasonally:
In every period, this magazine touches on some thematic topics. The Spring 2011 issue was dedicated to our women. I think that up to this point, of all the issues I read, this is the one from which I most benefitted.

There, Professor Çigdem Kağıtçıbaşı* made the most important assessments. She herself was the foremost in her field. Unfortunately, she passed away March 2017.

The title of her article is **"The Situation of Women in Turkey"**. Mrs. Kağıtçıbaşı was an expert on the topic of women's rights. Her explanation of the difference between an educated and an uneducated woman and analysis of the statistics are very revealing. When we look at the self-employed, in terms of women, all right as a country. It's a benefit that the Republic has given us.

When I am saying that the country's founding and aims were accurate, this is what I'm meaning. For example, we have a very high number of women dentists. There's not even a need for figures. There are women doctors and women architects. The number of women engineers isn't bad. The number of lawyers is quite high. But our problem is that in the 21st century, these are not possible.

Countries in the 21st century are needing to discuss very different things. I explained it earlier. Developed countries are engaged in a war against cancer, transhumanism, scientific and technological discoveries, amazing technologies such as nanotechnology and many other things.

Let me relate to you another anecdote from the same journal. *"Did you know that of 186 countries, the Turkey's rate of women's participation in the workforce is among the lowest 12 countries?"*

---

* http://mysite.ku.edu.tr/ckagit/

What does this mean? I'm sharing with you the first paragraph of Dr. Sumru Öz's article. For the rest of it, I will give the address where you can download from the internet a free copy of the journal for yourself to read.

"One of the most striking characteristics of the labor market in Turkey, whether you compare it with the OECD or the European and Central Asian countries, is that the participation of women in the workforce is among the lowest.

The data from the World Bank in 2008 shows that of 186 there are only 11 countries with lower rates of women employment: Egypt, Iraq, Jordan, Lebanon, Libya, Oman, Pakistan, Saudi Arabia, the Solomon Islands, Syria, and Yemen.

In addition, again according to the World Bank, to compare 2008 with 1980 shows that Turkey's rate of women employment is among the 23 countries whose rates dropped. In this period, the women participation rate in the workforce is declining from 32 to 25 percent. However, at the same time, the world's average for women labor force participation is showing a slight increase from 50 to 52 percent."

– **Could we have that address?**
– Of course, this contains some advice toward solutions. I recommend that everyone read it, especially women:

http://pr.ku.edu.tr/sites/pr.ku.edu.tr/files/kule-dergisi/arsiv/kule31/files/kule31.pdf

I actually wasn't planning to go into this topic. I'm trying to look at the issue more as a career consultant and speaker rather than an economist or an academician. But if the figures are deceiving, then in order to find reality, we have to put forth some effort.

Furthermore, it's important to do a great deal of identifying and paint the picture from the right perspective. The basic statistics that I used are from international institutions. What I want to say is this: "How much can a country develop if its women aren't in the workforce?"

"It's better to walk with a limp on the right road, then wander here and there with strong steps."

Augustinus

– **So, why do we need to look at unemployment numbers? What's the actual source? What do the criteria need to be?**
– The OECD* is headquartered in Paris, and in 2012, Turkey did the chairmanship. In Turkey, its founding caught the attention of a few reporters and academicians and same economic pages. Whether it's to students or to authorities, the value of the reports this institution produces cannot be explained.

– **Why is this?**
– I think the reason is this: It is said that until recent years whenever the OECD issued a report, in a merciless way, Turkey was not represented in the statistics but rather as a footnote. From my perspective, it means, "We didn't include Turkey because whether it's economic or other data, it would cause the OECD average to fall. That's why we didn't include them!"

This was a bad situation. Of course, this was not the case for all indicators but for some. Nevertheless, now Turkey is being included.

– **Who are members of this organization and what do they do?**
– The OECD member countries are: Austria, Belgium, Canada, Denmark, France, Germany, Luxembourg, Holland, Norway, Portugal, Spain, Greece, Iceland, Ireland, Italy, Sweden, Switzerland, Turkey, England, United States of America, Australia, Czech Republic, Finland, Hungary, Mexico, Japan, New Zealand, Poland, Slovak Republic, Slovenia, Israel, Estonia, Latvia, Chile and South Korea.**

---

* http://www.oecd.org/
** http://www.oecd.org/about/membersandpartners/

Now, do you understand why, until recently, Turkey was left out of some of the statistics? Because among these countries there are those who are very high on the development index. However, in recent times, there are some who have taken a hit. Consequently, now, it's okay if Turkey also causes the averages to go down.

Earlier we talked about the fact that some of these countries are the northern countries and are my favorites. The others are Mediterranean, and the far eastern countries are also star countries. You can see that, for Turkey, this is an association with quite high standards. As I see it, this is much more important than the "G20" and other similar formations; their figures and reports are much more important.

– **What do they do? What is the purpose of the organization?**
– The government representatives of the 35 countries that make up the OECD come together and work on difficulties and changes in the areas of the global economy, social topics, and the environment. By this means the governments are able to share their experiences and look together for solutions to common problems. With the forthcoming results, they are able to make comparisons among the countries.

You can see that the OECD is like a **good litmus test**. It serves as a remarkable economic laboratory. For example, in 2007 Turkey, along with Mexico and the oceanic region, was characterized as one making economic leaps. Actually, since 2008 and 2009, the outlook began to take a bad turn. I read the comments that the OECD made for 2008 and 2009. These are very important, because now from here you can see what the general signs are for a crisis.

– **Are there signs?**
– There are. Look at what the report says, I'm reading a portion of the report summary:

> "According to the figures that were given from the study, in the OECD area, the employment growth numbers in 2006 were

1.7 percent, whereas in 2007 there was a 1.5 percent decline.

Again, in the OECD area, the labor supply increases in 2006 and 2007 were 1.1 and 1 percent, respectively. In the data from the OECD study, it's evident that employment rose faster than labor supply in most OECD member countries. In the OECD area in 2006 while 34.1 million people were looking for work, in 2007 this number was reduced to 31.9 million. In other terms, the unemployment rate fell from 6 to 5.6 percent.

In 2008 and 2009 it is expected that these ratios will change in the same manner with a rise in employment (0.7%, 0.5%) and labor supply (0.8%, 0.8%). In the OECD area, it is expected that the declines in unemployment ratios that have been experienced in the last period will be reversed. The unemployment count in 2008 is expected to rise by one million and by 2 million in 2009. If this happens, the average unemployment ratio in the OECD area in 2009 will again reach its level it was in 2006 of 6%."

– **Can we say that these figures were realized?**
– It turned out to be worse than what's above. You know that 2008 and 2009 were catastrophic years. The disaster has not yet passed. Because it's not the heart of the matter.

However, what I want to explain is different. I am determining that the OECD, who was nearly able to say that in 2008 and 2009 "a big crisis is coming", is better able to see the coming years than rating institutions and other authorities.

It means that in this environment of misinformation and faulty managing, the institution that can most be trusted is the OECD and its reports.

– **At this point, what is the OECD saying about unemployment?**
– Look, the most important thing about unemployment is not the answer to the question, "How many people are looking for work?" You can manipulate this question as much as you want: Have you looked for work in the last 3 months? Have you looked for work in the last 6 months? Have you worked in the last 3 hours? Actually, the answer that must be sought is to this question: **How much a person is free or can work but isn't look-**

ing for work / is not able to look/is not able to find even if looking or is tired of looking and is forced to give up?
- **At this point...**
- At this point, the primary criterion that must be looked at is the ratio of **labor force participation**. If this ratio is high then it means that things are going well. If this rate is low, most particularly if it's under 50 percent then the situation is grave. If we add the on top of this the unemployment rate, an accurate formula forms: **the labor force participation rate + the unemployment rate. The two together show you something.**

- Where is Turkey in workforce participation?
- Turkey hovers above and below 50 percent. Sometimes it declines and sometimes it rises. It's confusing. I think the reason for this is unreported employment.

In my hand, I have the "Monthly Employment Report" which analyzes the past years' last quarters. It was put out in March 2013 by the Republic of Turkey Ministry of Development, Directorate General for Social Sectors and Coordination, and the Department of Employment and Work Life. This is what's written on the third page:

> *"The labor force participation rate for 2012 compared to the same period in the previous year rising from 48.5 to 50 percent, the workforce rose to 27 million 556 thousand people. The working age population in Turkey is above 55 million."*

These are the government's figures for the same time. Before our conversation ends, according to the last report, the number of those able to be employed rose to **30 million 855 thousand.*** Here, rather than the figures, the important thing is the primary philosophy of approach.

Two years or 5 years later the figures will change. However, the message will be the same message. Unfortunately, the message will remain relevant... The important thing is one figure:

---

*   Feb 2017

Of the whole population, what is the workforce participation rate?

Source: http://www.tuik.gov.tr/HbGetirHTML.do?id=24 941

(TSI calculates the periodical employment results from "active 3-month periods". This report covers January, February and March of the 2017 period.)

According to the figures of this TSI poll, **"but be careful, according to some polls and calculations"**, we are able to provide work for 26 million 956 thousand people. In this case, according to the government, there are approximately 3,9 million unemployed.

These figures based on poll's questions may show the seasonal changes in the workforce participation rates, the increase of the working age population, and repercussions of the economic crisis. But the most important thing is the nature of the survey's questions.

– **So then is 50 percent of this country not working?**
– As I explained earlier, we can't know this for sure. This is due to too many unregistered workers. And I reckon we don't know the reality of it. It is said that a number of unregistered workers are nearly 32,8 percent of total workforce. It is said! I'm not sure how clear this is.

Now in the OECD, this is based on the labor force participation rate (a rough estimate and variable). It's best for us to regard the OECD's figures. The most trustworthy reference point that we have is this organization's figures.

Yes, according to this perspective and the government's acceptance of the of it, there is no relation with the jobs of 50 percent of the working age population.

– **So, for this entry what is the OECD average?**
– The "average" in OECD countries' of the working age population who have a job or make up the active workforce (population between the ages of 15 and 64) is **71,3** percent.* The world aver-

---

* https://data.oecd.org/emp/labour-force-participation-rate.htm

age is **62.8 percent**.* Turkey's last average for these ages group is **56,8** percent.

Like the OECD countries that I listed earlier 71,3 is the percentage, we could reach. Of course, some are lower and some are higher. But no matter how you multiply, divide and break it down, figures close to these will result. These points are a full **"14,5"** points above Turkey's. According to this, the unemployment figures need to be recalculated.

– How is that?

– Look...

Since the OECD labor force participation rate averages, 71,3 percent or you could say of the working age population, 71,3 people are working and since it is maintained that they could work, this rate provides an average that we can use as a reference.

When making our calculations we must do it in this way: if of the population that is able to work (that is 59 million 567 thousand) and 71.3 are really in the workforce or have affirmed that they want to be, then how many should be working?

Let me calculate for you: 42.471.271 people should be working or in the population able to work.

So, we're insisting on using the OECD average. But we have a working population of approximately 30 million 855 thousand potential and according to the government, of these 26 million 956 thousand people are working. We have about 3,9 million unemployed people. According to the government, our average unemployment rate is in the 12,9 percent range.

But there's a problem...

Our population that is able to work is not 30,85 million, it is 59,5 million.

If our values were up to the OECD standard average of 71,3 percent, the size of the workforce wouldn't be 30 million and 855 thousand (as in 56,8 percent of 59 million 567 thousand people), it would have reached 42 million 471 thousand.

---

* http://data.worldbank.org/indicator/SL.TLF.CACT.ZS

Since Turkey, in reality, during the same period could provide jobs for 26 million 956 thousand people, the numbers of unemployed also instead of reaching 3,9 million would be 15,5 million. In this case, the unemployment rate would be 36,49 percent.

At this point in order to not share more mathematical data, I won't give the European workforce participation numbers or, especially, Spain and Italy's workforce participation numbers. I don't want to confuse people too much. This is now how I figure it. The OECD is doing the calculations. The OECD's published formal figures are at this level.

At one time, the OECD gave the figure of 31.36 for Turkey. Because of fluctuating factors such as the youth population coming up and the people who surpass the age of 64, we may not see the same figures each year.

– **Earlier you had actually had said that the figure was higher, in the 30th percentile. Are you referring to this?**
– That's exactly what I want to say. I am asserting that the existing figures that are put forth, with this logic, should at least be multiplied by 3.

This figure doesn't change just for us, for all of the OECD countries, when based on OECD figures very different calculated figures emerge. The countries that are currently in crisis or in difficult situations such as Greece and Spain, the rates could change. Just like currently in Spain which is in crisis (I can't stand it; I have to say it.), the labor force participation rate is at the **75,5** percent level. Think about this...

– **At that rate, this means that Turkey has good odds. When the labor force participation rate is low, unemployment doesn't increase astronomically. Isn't this good?**
– Nice logic. I want to add this: Of these countries, Turkey had the largest population of youth and of those who are able to work. However, you look at it, there's an abnormal distortion. Let me answer your question this way: no, that's not the case...

Turkey has two big problems:

One, our women labor force participation rates are very, very low.

Turkey's women labor force participation rates are not accurate due to working off the books. We don't know how much women who are field workers, workers in homes, housecleaners, those who give private classes and others in the service sector are working or not working.

But our average value that pulls the percentage to 56,8 percent is the women labor force participation rate. According to some sources, the women labor force participation rate is 25-28 percent. According to TSI is 36 percent range (Feb 2017).

Earlier, I mentioned to you the "Kule" magazine. There you can find many articles and essays that support Dr. Sumru Öz's article. The readers might read the same information, but, I reiterate, this is basic information.

For example, Dr. Sumru Öz declares that the women labor force participation rate is 25 percent, however, Talip Aktaş from "World" magazine says it's 28 percent. As I've said, this figure is different with everyone. But it's in this range. I'm relating to you the last part of a July 2012 analysis from World magazine written by Talip Aktaş:

> "The women labor force scene isn't encouraging...
>
> To be far behind developed countries and many developing countries in labor force participation, in essence, is due to the women labor force participation being at such an incredibly low level. It is possible to have a qualitative increase of women in the workforce. Outside of primitive, agriculturally based countries in Africa, of developed countries, there isn't one that has women labor force rate falling below 50 percent. The average rate of women in the labor force in developed countries is in the 60th percentile, above the 50 percent rate in developing countries. Again, while excluding the countries experiencing the specific situation of famine, at its core workforce quality reveals a pattern that is directly related to the level of educated women in the labor force.
>
> In the countries where educated women labor force participation is high, the women labor force participation also

reaches a high level. In the current scene, the linear relationship between the level of development and general labor force participation and especially women's participation in the labor force shows that Turkey has a long road ahead. In other words, unless women don't make up half of the labor force, then the expectations for progress that are being made don't appear likely."

– **As things are, we must increase the population rate of women who work or want to work.**
– Yes, but while doing this, we must take care of unreported employment. Actually, every type of economic system and structure is indexed. If we can arrive at a situation of being registered, it becomes easier to control life. Otherwise, we continue to fish in murky waters.

I'd like to commend the valuable Professor Osman Altuğ.

– **He's struggled against the unregistered economy, hasn't he?**
– You said it...

I had an opportunity to meet with him. It was the year 2008. Marmara University called on me to make a speech. At that time, I was the manager of an American company.

Not actually coming as a representative of that company, understanding that I would explain reality to the students, before the seminar he showered me with praise. I clearly remember what he said, *"Come and explain to the youth the realities of work life."* Professor Osman was accurate in what he said from the very first day. But we generally did the opposite of what he said.

He has a very old book in Turkey called **"The Unregistered Economy"**. I read it many years ago. I recommend to young people and those interested in the topic to at least search for and find it at the used book stores.

There's also a great book on **"The unregistered Economy and The Fast-moving Consumer Goods Sector"**. It's a book written by Professor Metin Ercan in 2006. The book's publisher is the Active Approach to the Consumer Association. I highly recommend this book. There is important information especially concerning employment and unregistered employment.

In the end, I've have found that there are two people who are experts in this field in Turkey: Professor Osman Altuğ and Professor Metin Ercan.

* * *

"Better to be ignorant of a matter than half know it."

Publilius Syrus*

---

* Publilius Syrus (fl. 85–43 BC), was a Latin writer of sententiae. He was a Syrian who was brought as a slave to Italy, but by his wit and talent he won the favour of his master, who freed and educated him. Publilius' name, due to early medieval palatalization of 'l' between two 'i's, is often presented by manuscripts (and some printed editions) in corrupt form as 'Publius'. (Source: Wikipedia)

2. WORK LIFE IS MADE UP OF PROCEDURE!

— In your seminars you give many explanations, for example, you explain what "working on Büyükdere Street" is or isn't. I'd like to make our conversation longer since there are still many other topics that we didn't discuss, but again after asking about a few of the topics I am curious about, I need to end this conversation of which I'm not able to get enough.

— Yes, very good. You remembered. What does it mean "**to work on Büyükdere Street?**"

Look... Büyükdere Street is Turkey's most important street. Like İstiklal Street and Bağdat Street, there are numerous other streets that have become symbols of Istanbul and Turkey.

İstiklal Street is Turkey's most valuable symbolic street in a touristic, cultural, social and political sense. There is no doubt about that.

İstiklal and Taksim square formed the basis for the **Gezi events.*** Why? Because it's a symbol of Turkey. However, from a work life perspective, Büyükdere Street is number one.

To start with, Büyükdere Street is a long street. It's actually bigger than the borders that are assumed and its background is very rich. To put it roughly, it is a street that extends from Mecidiyeköy, starting from Cevahir Shopping Center to the Sarıyer Hacıosman slope. In fact, the road that is called Bahçeköy road

---
* https://en.wikipedia.org/wiki/Gezi_Park_protests

going toward Kilyos, the road that goes all the way into the Belgrad Forest is named "Büyükdere Bahçeköy Road". You can see that it is a very long road and street.

If I remember correctly, it was asserted in one calculation that the produced total value in Turkey or expressed differently, the 5 percent of the Gross National Product is produced on Büyükdere Street.

This is an old adjustment. If a new calculation were to be made, I contend that this figure could easily be at the 10 percent level. In fact, it could even be higher than 10 percent. Actually, Turkey doesn't exactly know what this street is and isn't.

I say that...

If you say, "I work in the center. I'm a worker at the hub." there's only one response to this. There aren't 50 responses.

To work in the center means to work on "Büyükdere Street".

If you don't work on this street or you don't work on a nearby street or neighborhood, it means you don't work in the center.

A country or a city has one center. It's not possible to have 2 or 3. This needs to be made clear to start with. **Büyükdere Street isn't just İstanbul's, it's Turkey's center.**

– **Aren't all the banks here?**
– If it were just the banks, fine...

The Istanbul Stock Exchange Market, the headquarters of our largest holdings and even the headquarters for the government and finance are here.

There is a building that belongs to the Ministry of Finance here. Where is the Large Taxpayer's Office which is connected to the Directorate General for Inspection for the Ministry of Finance? Where is it? Right beside the Kanyon Mall.

Why? Because nearly every important large taxpayer is on this street.

The İş Bank General Management, Şişecam General Management, Yapı Kredi Bank General Management, Akbank General Management, Eczacıbaşı Group, Sabancı Towers, Istanbul Stock Exchange Market, ING Bank General Management, Şekerbank General Management, Vakıfbank General Management additional buildings, Turkey's largest pharmaceutical firm Abdi İbrahim İlaç firması, Glaxo Smith Kline, Sanofi Aventis, general management for world pharmaceutical giants such as Roche, PepsiCo International General Management, Kanyon Shopping Center, İstinye Park Shopping Center, Metrocity Shopping Center, İstanbul Technical University, some departments of Yıldız Technical University, Beykent University, numerous hotels, etc.

Thousands of company headquarters that I don't want to list at this time or their representative offices in Turkey are on this street. Nearly all are here except Koç Group and some companies also that aren't able to find space or have high expenses. I can't think of a similar concentration on one street in the world. Normally the concentrations are in districts. But there is no other place that carries this type load.

– **Is everything very glorious here?**
– That is the essential issue! Unfortunately, there is a style of work on that street that has become a bad example to Turkey. The truth is, of course, that this is not a culture particular to this street: "Plaza Cult" is actually is sickness (Cult: religion; French-based; an event or a film with excessive attention).

At first glance, it seems appealing to work on these types of streets.

Look, I worked in a building directly in the middle of this street for 7 years. This is a 26-floor tower that doesn't even have any windows that open.

When you look at it from the outside, you say, "What a beautiful building." It's true. But what kind of building? It's a building where not one window can open and inside the likelihood of your getting sick in the winter months is very high. As for summer, the normal amount of coolness harms people.

Especially women workers have a very hard time **because the heat of a women's and men's bodies are different.** Or let's say that their senses of heat are different. Most of the time the buildings are adjusted to men's sense of heat.

People are cooped up in these buildings for 8-10 hours, and later this we call that work life. This is an unwholesome system.

Due to intangible reasons, I like Büyükdere Street where I spent my childhood. However, due to physical reasons and the times when I look from a rational frame, I can't say that it's an ideal place.

– But today everyone wants to work on this street...
– Rightly so, since just like I explained just a moment ago, all the large firms are here. I find people's desires to work here very natural. I also greatly desired it. In fact, if needed I'd work there again, but it's not an ideal environment. I'd like to go deeper into the topic of the **"Plaza Cult"** and its harm in another conversation.

The second disadvantage of this street is a place where there are not enough sports and cultural activities are not held.

You are going to ask if the other places are different. Here, the important thing is this: this street is not just Turkey's, but it is numbered among the world's streets. In this sense, there need to be places where nearly every worker, upon leaving work in the evening, can easily do sports or, without going too far, on the same street go to plays and concerts. If it had these characteristics, then workers would better be able to tolerate the stress here.

Furthermore, one last word...

One of the biggest mistakes in this area is that when each of the malls was being made, there needed to be a license requirement for them to build something like a theater and a concert area.

In this sense, I'd like to congratulate Cevahir Shopping Center and the İş Towers. Cevahir, while first being build set aside two theaters for the State Theater. The İş Towers making a world-class concert hall became a center for the arts. The Zorlu Center and Uniq Istanbul projects are also important concert centers. I congratulate them.

– I understand. I'd like to talk about this topic in another detailed conversation. I want to come to a different topic. When describing the Turkish work life, you mention "operationalism" What does this mean?
– Look... This doesn't just apply to our country. This is a global problem. I mentioned it earlier. How interesting that the work

world isn't expecting you to be creative or for you to do interesting things.

Bosses and companies want to see functional personalities around them. This world is a world of the procedure. This country has become a country of the procedure. In this country, it is expected of you that you will do certain functions. It's not important that you receive a super education. Actually, it's not important that you know 3 or 4 languages. There are essentially a few things you must do.

Know how to use well basic programs such as Excel / Word, SAP, and ORACLE.

However, what did we say? The path to real professionalism passes through specialization. Good, but in this system, work life cuts the branch that you climbed onto. It prevents people from specializing better and deeper and sees them as a processing machine.

– **Have we all become robots?**
– Exactly. Now each of us is a robot. It doesn't matter if you have broad experience. The system first is expecting you to have the very good processing power.
In this sense, work life is in a stranded position.

– **Why is that?**
– At the basis of it there are two reasons:

First, like I explained earlier, now production isn't important. Productional procedures and real sales and marketing tied to it don't happen as much. Rather, **financial procedures** have become important. **In this sense, more finance means more procedures.**

In these sorts of times, financiers and accountants are more important since more work comes to them in a larger processing environment...

Secondly, the unpreventable importance of computerization and the subsequent elevated, super information accumulation that happens. In order to be able to process this information, there is a need for a great number of workers.

In this sense, before developing into a discipline, the Turkish business world came under its influence and was thoroughly wrapped in a procedure-based setting. Conversely, the work world doesn't want you to be a person who is an extremely good leader, to believe in your work and have the greatest personality. At some companies, they want you to do the work of not 2, not 3 but of 4 people.

– **We're in a depressing situation...**
– Exactly. At this time, a large portion of Turkish society is in depression. Workers are depressed, non-workers are also depressed due to unemployment and other general concerns. But how interesting that a large portion of the society doesn't even know that it is in depression.

– **Is this tied to violence against women?**
– Definitely...**Hopelessness, as we mentioned earlier,** is root factor in violence against women, general intolerance, and other problems.

In the last 15 years in this country, the consumption of depression medicines has increased at an incredible rate. No one has researched the critical reasons for it. We are trying to control the sale of medicines. But this mustn't be forgotten: even if you outlaw the medicines, without doing away with the underlying factors triggering the buying of the medicines, then you can't hinder the sale of depression medicines.

This isn't possible. Sooner or later, they will be sold, even if it's illegal.

– **You're saying the situation is grave...**
– I think the situation is especially grave in Turkey as well as in the Mediterranean countries that I mentioned earlier. Because in these types of countries, you become depressed if you work or if you don't work. The result doesn't change.

Especially those who live in Istanbul, they become depressed merely going out into the traffic. Even just this by itself is enough.

* * *

www.ingramcontent.com/pod-product-compliance
Lightning Source LLC
Chambersburg PA
CBHW050203230526
45470CB00001B/215